Belleville Ontario Book 1 in Colour Photos, Saving Our History One Photo at a Time

Photography
by Barbara Raué
2016

Series Name:
Cruising Ontario

Book 163: Belleville Book 1

Cover photo: 221 John Street, Page 31

Series Name: Cruising Ontario
The Authority on Saving Our History One Photo at a Time in colour photos

Books Available in Alphabetical Order:
Aberfoyle, Acton, Alton, Amherstburg, Ancaster, Arthur, Aylmer, Ayr, Bloomingdale, Brantford, Burlington, Caledon, Caledonia, Cambridge, Clifford, Conestogo, Delhi, Dorchester to Aylmer, Drayton, Drumbo, Dundas, Eden Mills, Elmira, Elora, Essex, Fergus, Guelph, Hagersville, Hamilton, Hanover, Harriston, Hespeler, Jarvis, Kingston, Kingsville, Kitchener, Linwood, Listowel, London, Lucknow, Mono, Mount Forest, Neustadt, New Hamburg, Niagara-on-the-Lake, Oakville, Orangeville, Orillia, Owen Sound, Palmerston, Peterborough, Petrolia, Port Elgin, Preston, Rockwood, Sarnia, Seaforth, Sheffield, Shelburne, Simcoe, Southampton, St. Jacobs, St. Marys, St. Thomas, Stoney Creek, Stratford, Thamesford, Tillsonburg, Waterdown, Waterford, Waterloo, Welland, Wellesley, Windsor, Wingham, Woodstock

Other Books by Barbara Raue

Coins of Gold

Arrows, Indians and Love

The Life and Times of Barbara
Volume 1: Inventions That Have Enhanced My Life
Volume 2: Entertainment That I Have Enjoyed
Volume 3: East Coast Trips
Volume 4: Olympics Have Always Intrigued Me
Volume 5: Wonders of the World
Volume 6: Caribbean Cruises We Have Enjoyed
Volume 7: Animals
Volume 8: Storms and Other Major Disasters in My Lifetime
Volume 9: Wars, Terrorist Attacks and Major Disasters

The Cromwell Family Book

Laura Secord Discovered

Daddy Where Are You?

Montana Series
Book 1: Montana Dream
Book 2: Life on the Montana Frontier
Book 3: Montana to Boston and Back

Visit Barbara's website to view all of her books
http://barbararaue.ca

Table of Contents

The Bay of Quinte Yacht Club was formed in October 1876 with full yachting activities commencing the following season. The first Lake Yacht Racing Associate races were a series of regattas held in Toronto, Oswego, Kingston, and Belleville. The Belleville Regatta was sailed on August 12, 1885 in Big Bay. Informal sailing races were held on the Bay of Quinte during the 1930s. In 1978, the Bay of Quinte Yacht Club played an active role in the City of Belleville's Centennial Year Celebrations.

Belleville is a city located at the mouth of the Moira River on the Bay of Quinte in southeastern Ontario. It was the site of a village of the Mississaugas in the eighteenth century. It was settled by United Empire Loyalists beginning in 1784. It was named Belleville in honor of Lady Arabella Gore in 1816, after a visit to the settlement by Sir Francis Gore and his wife.

It is known as the "friendly city" because it offers big city amenities along with small town friendliness, and a pleasing mixture of the historic and modern.

Belleville became an important railway junction with the completion of the Grand Trunk Railway in 1855. In 1858 the iron bridge over the Moira River at Bridge Street was constructed. Belleville's beautiful High Victorian Gothic city hall was built in 1872 to house the public market and administrative offices.

Due to its location near Lake Ontario, its climate is moderated by cooling hot summer days and warming cold days during the fall and winter.

Procter & Gamble, Kellogg's, Redpath, and Sears are corporations operating in Belleville. There are many other manufacturing sector companies which operate within the City of Belleville, including Sprague Foods, Sigma Stretch Film Canada, Reid's Dairy, and Parmalat Canada - Black Diamond Cheese Division, to name a few.

Belleville has an excellent yacht harbor, which is a picturesque stopping point for Great Lakes sailors and a favorite launch for sports fishing enthusiasts after walleye, pike and bass. Beautiful music chimes can be heard all year long from the City Hall clock tower, overlooking the new civic square and Farmers Market. Walking, biking and rollerblading can be enjoyed on the Bayshore and Riverfront Trails.

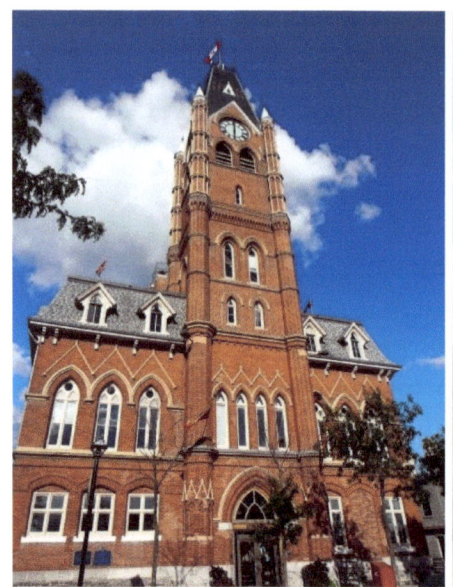
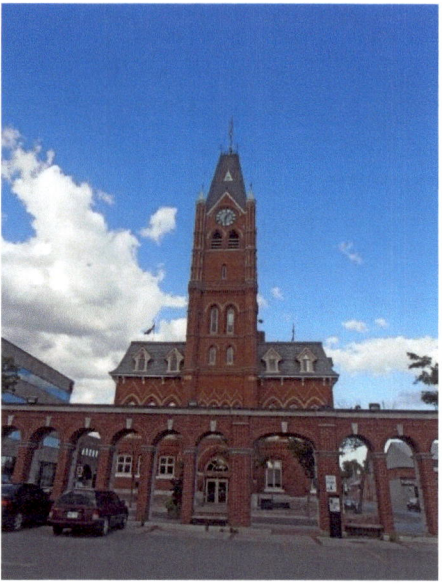

169 Front Street - Town Hall - designed by local architect John D. Evans and built in 1872-73 by contractor John Forin in High Victorian Gothic Revival style - brick and limestone building with tall lancet windows on the second floor with mullions dividing the windows in two with simple tracery in the arches, a bell-cast mansard roof with dormers, a massive 144-foot clock tower with octagonal buttresses, four large illuminated clock faces and cast iron railings and weathervanes

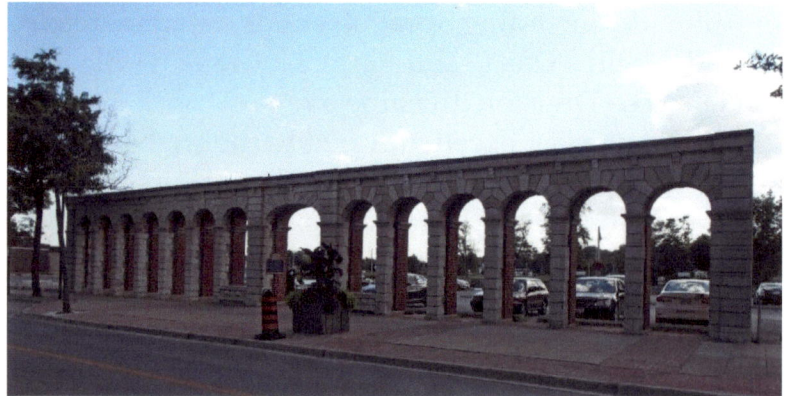

Site of the Bogart-Carman Building – John Forin built it in 1871 in the Renaissance Revival style as a retail and office building with a carriageway in the centre – daily and weekly newspapers published here - the first floor stone façade was salvaged in 1988 after the building collapsed

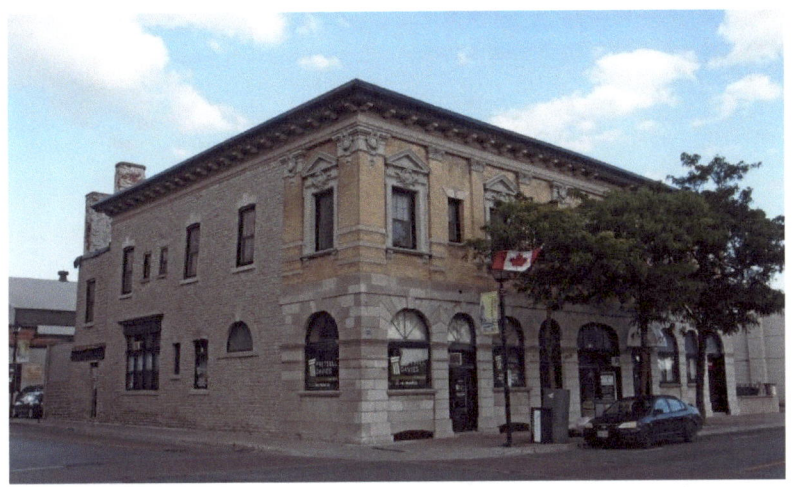

155-163 Front Street – Pretsell Davies, lawyers – decorative cornice with brackets, decorative window hoods with pediments, pilasters with decorative capitals

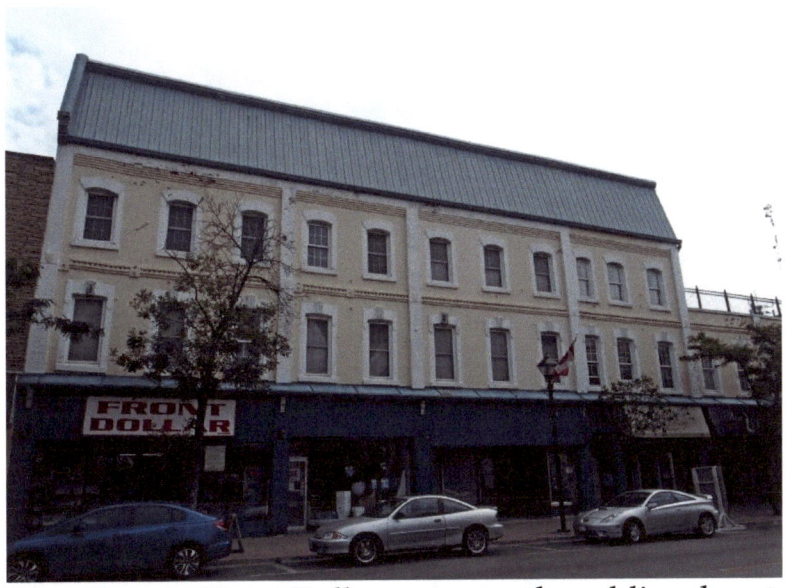

242 Front Street – Front Dollar – saw tooth molding, keystones and voussoirs, pilasters

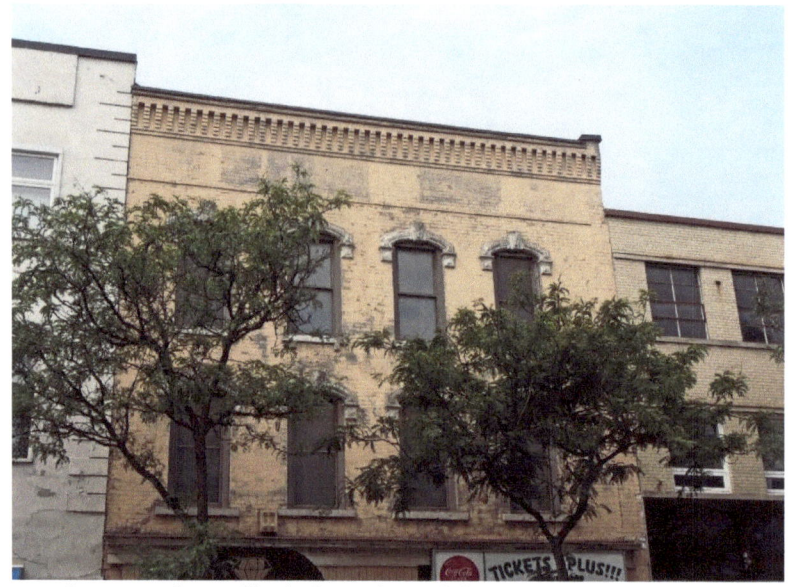

Front Street – bevelled dentil molding, window molds with keystones

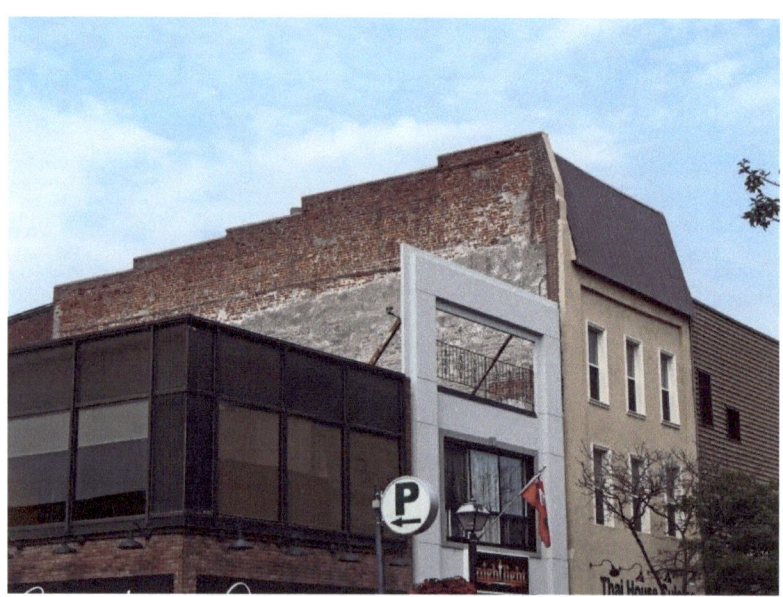

230 Front Street – Tai House

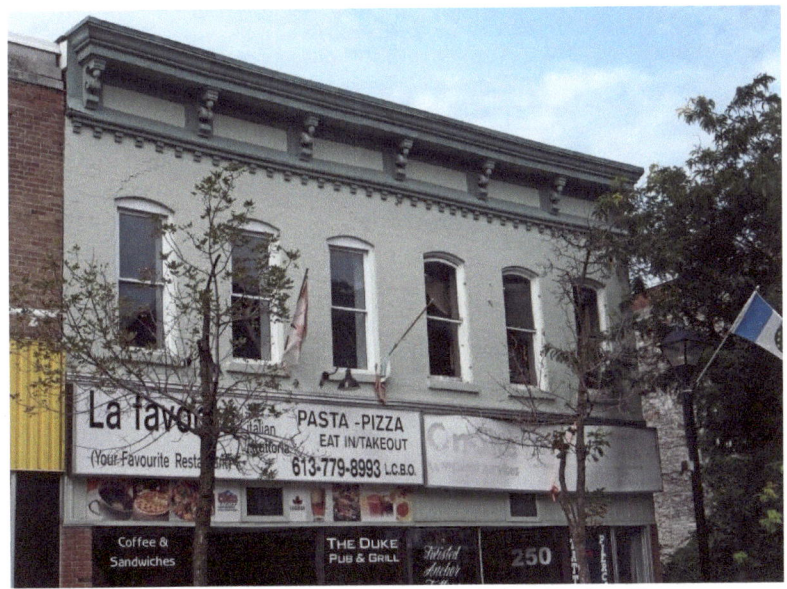

248-250 Front Street – La Favorita, The Duke Restaurant – cornice brackets, dentil molding

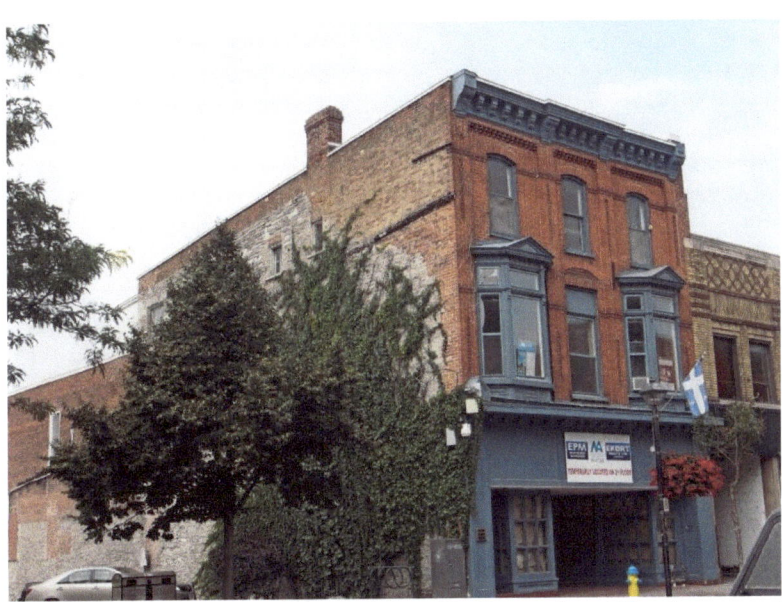

258 Front Street – Corby-Caldwell-Greenley Block - cornice brackets, saw tooth molding, bay windows, pilasters, banding – heritage property

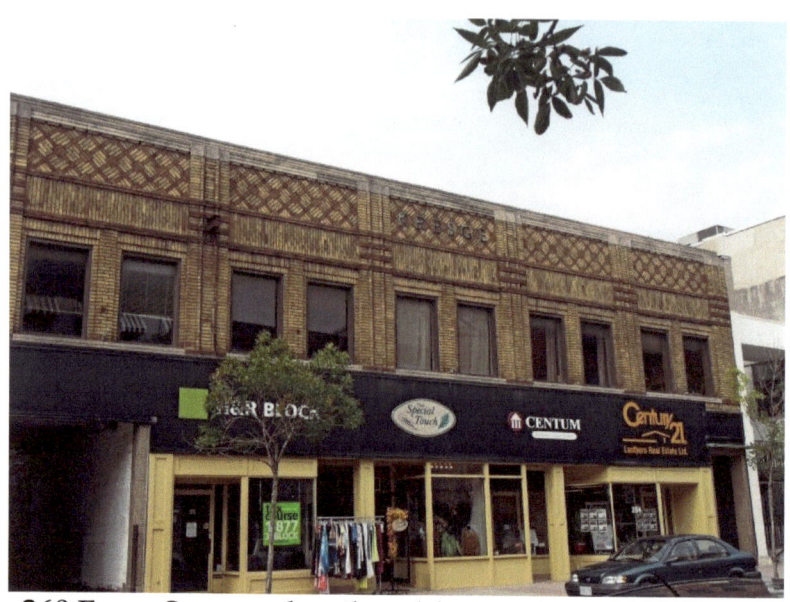

260 Front Street – dentil molding, pilasters, banding, dichromatic patterning

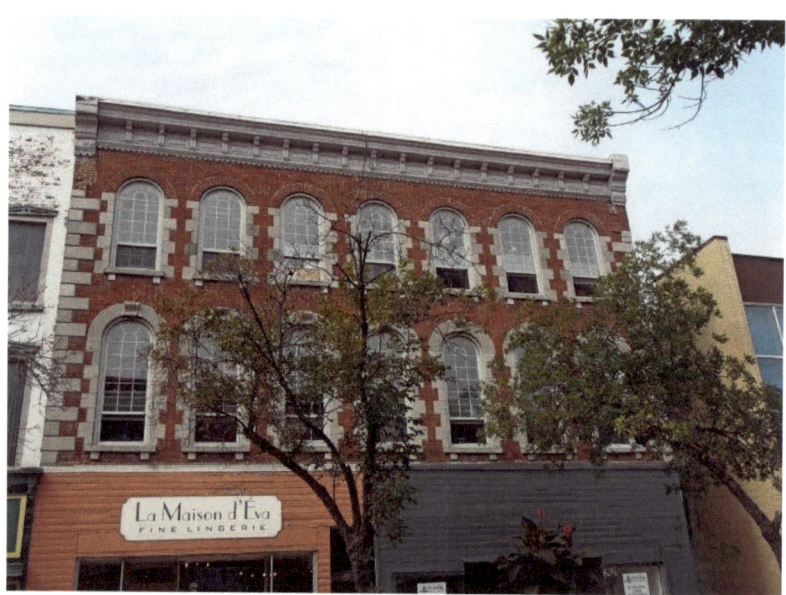

280 Front Street – La Maison d'Eva - decorative cornice with brackets, window voussoirs and quoining

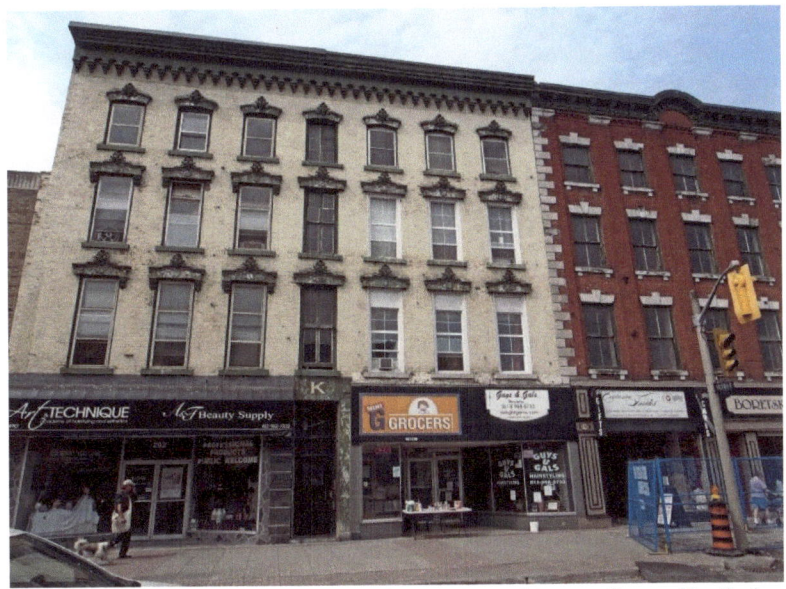

296 Front Street – Guys & Gals Hairstyling – bevelled dentil molding, window hoods

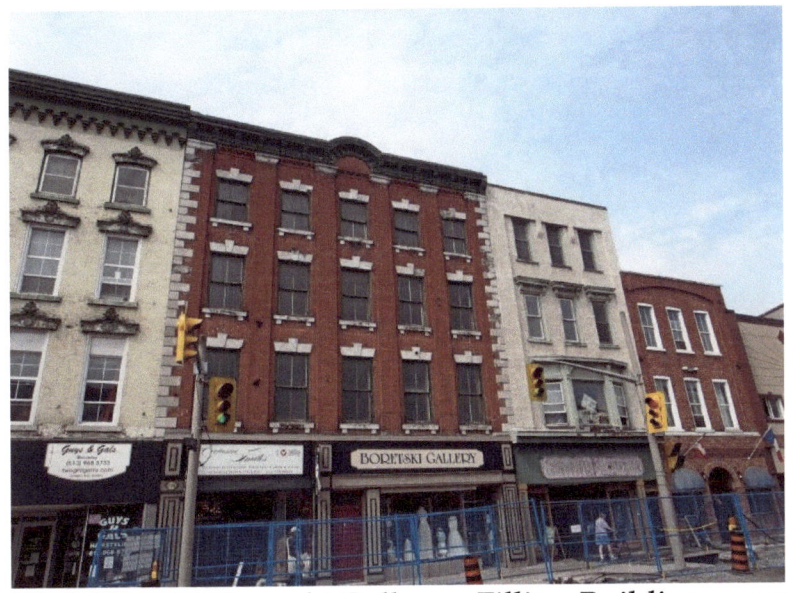

300 Front Street – Boretski Gallery – Filliter Building – cornice brackets, dentil molding, pilasters, keystones, corner quoins

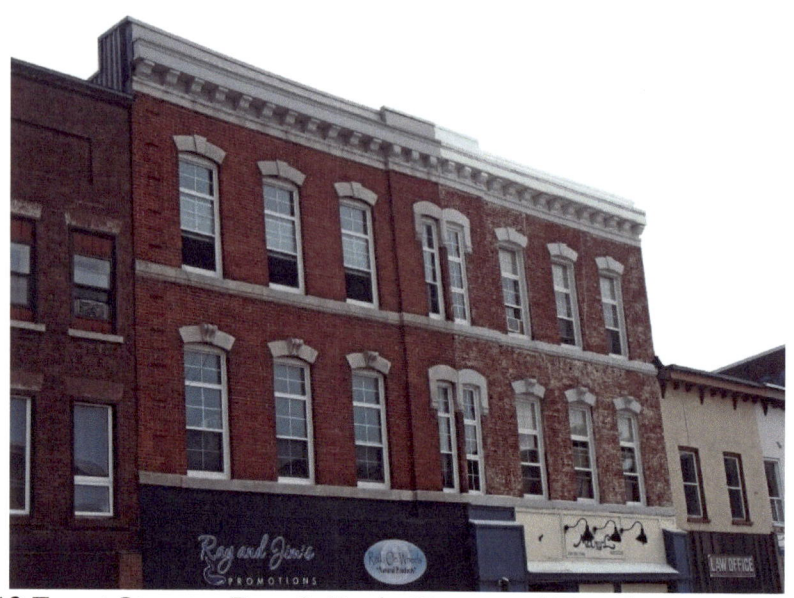

313 Front Street – Ray & Jim's Signs and Trophies – cornice brackets, string courses

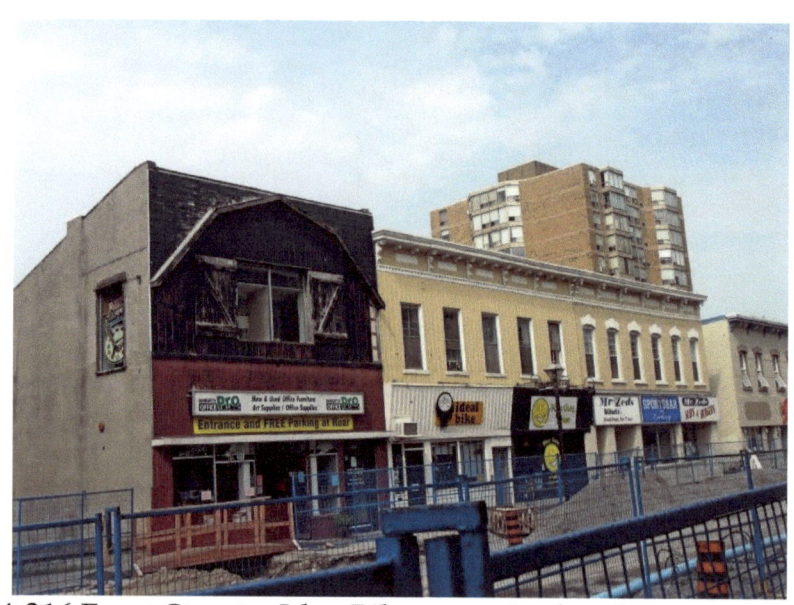

314-316 Front Street – Idea Bike – cornice brackets, saw tooth molding

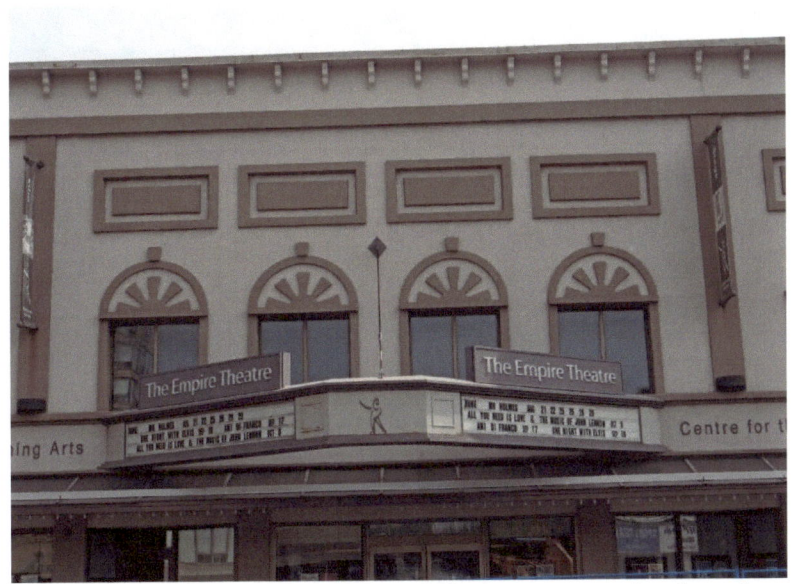

321 Front Street – The Empire Theatre – cornice brackets,
dichromatic plaster

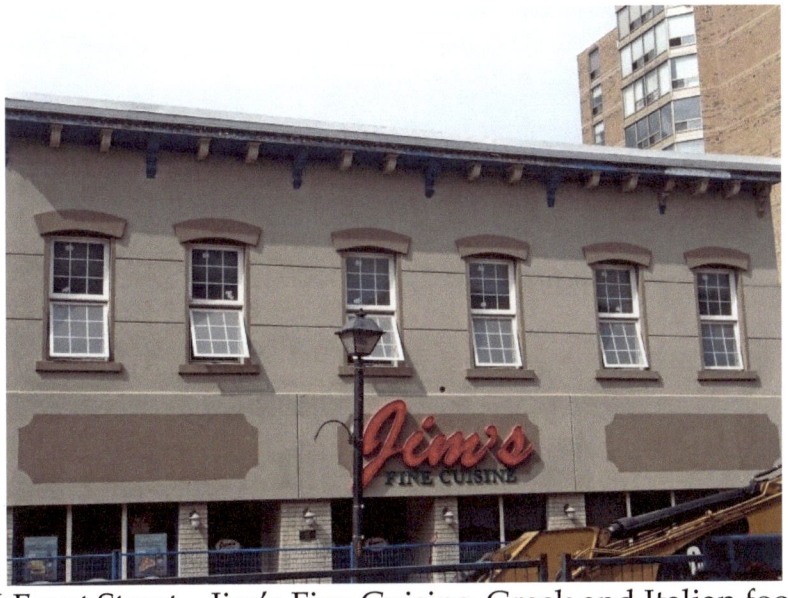

326 Front Street – Jim's Fine Cuisine, Greek and Italian food –
cornice brackets

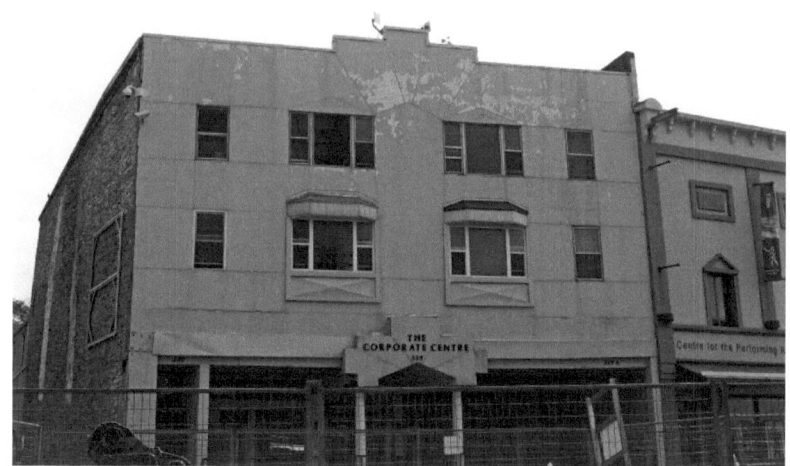

329 Front Street – The Corporate Centre

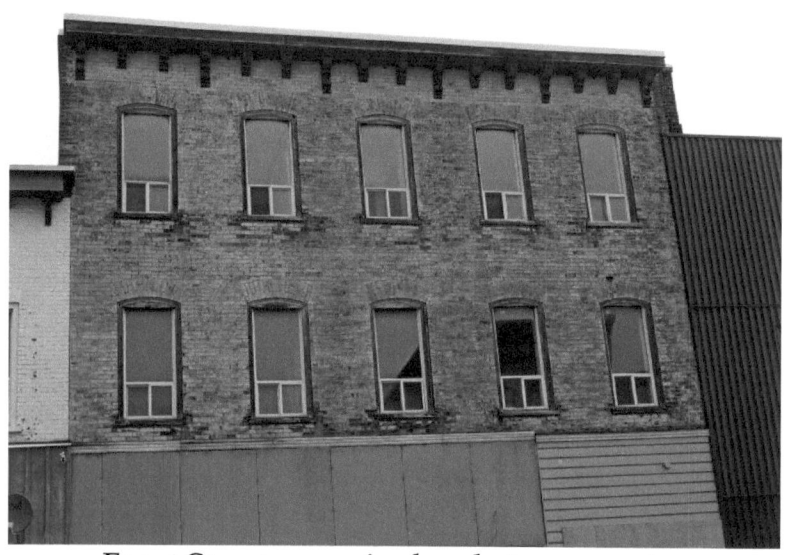

Front Street – cornice brackets, voussoirs

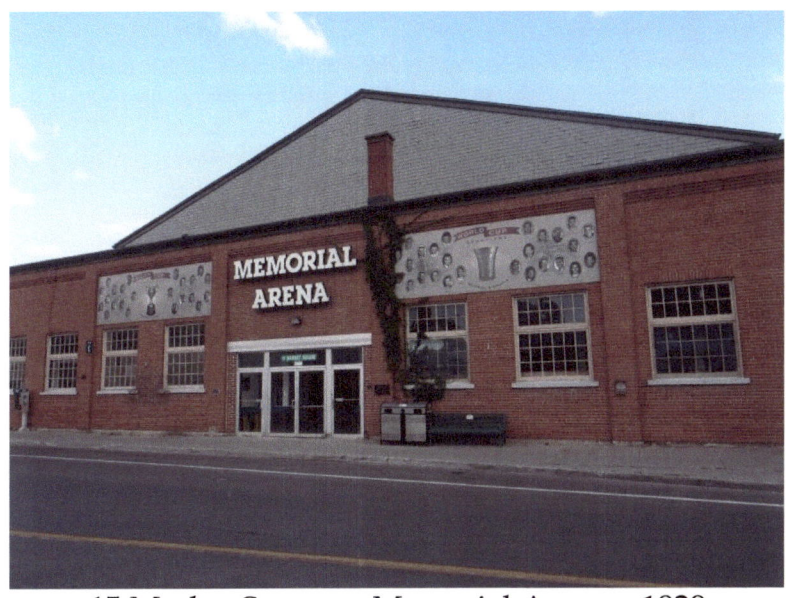

15 Market Square – Memorial Arena – 1929

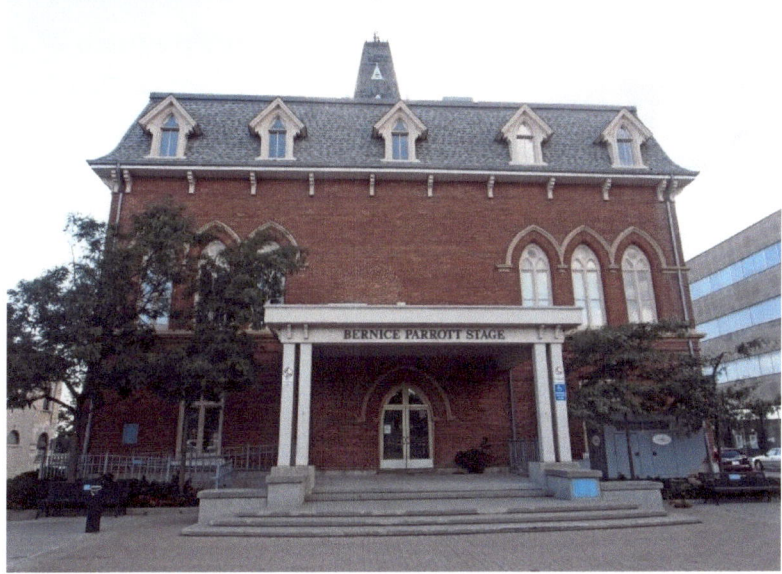

Market Square – Bernice Parrott Stage

The Market Square has played a major role in Belleville's history. The original town plan in 1816 reserved land for a market.

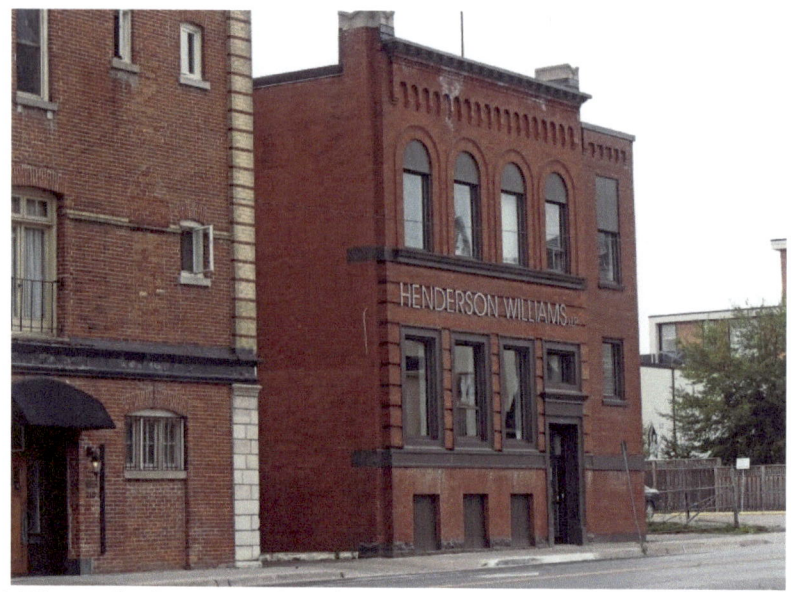

214 Pinnacle Street – Henderson Williams LLP Barristers and Solicitors – saw tooth and bevelled dentil molding

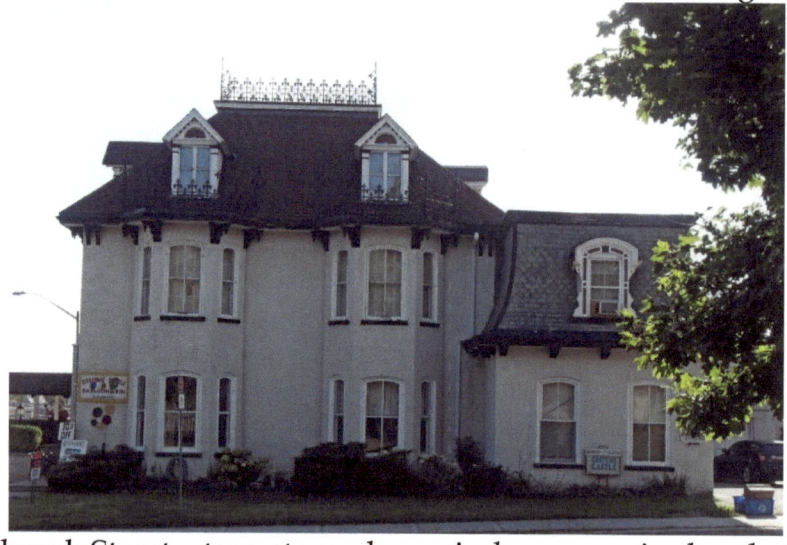

Church Street – two-storey bay windows, cornice brackets, dormers with iron cresting, widow's walk on rooftop with iron cresting; 2½-storey section has a hipped roof; 2-storey part has a mansard roof

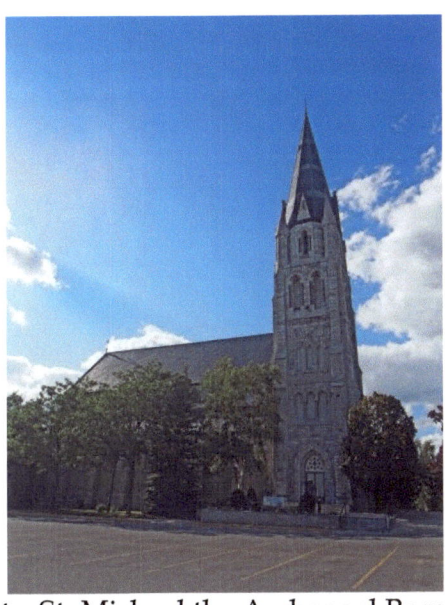

296 Church Street – St. Michael the Archangel Roman Catholic Church – 1905 - Gothic style - built of rusticated stone – buttresses, rose window

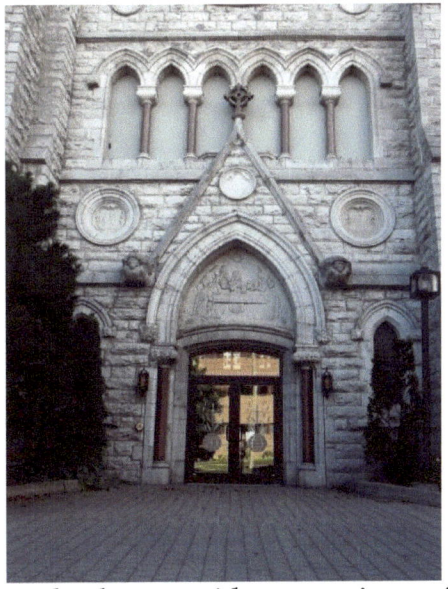

Portal with engaged columns with composite capitals supporting the arch with *The Lord's Supper* sculpted on the tympanum; engaged columns on the arched lancet windows

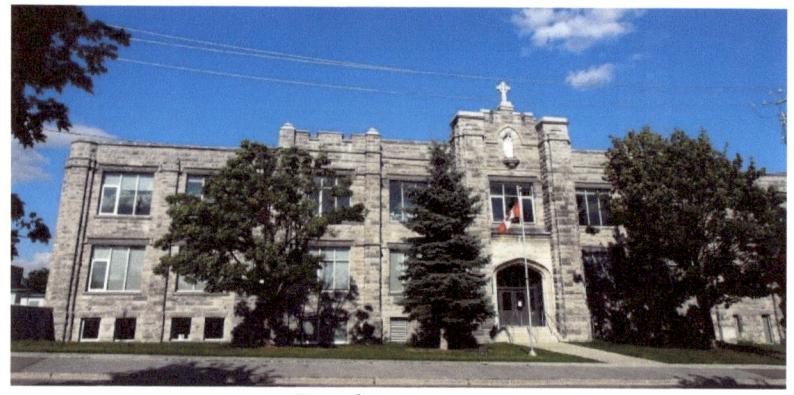

Battlementing

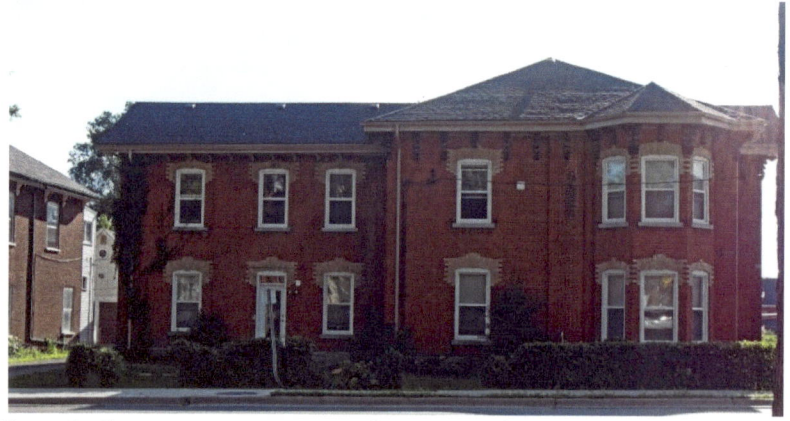

Church Street – two-storey bay window, cornice brackets, dichromatic voussoirs and keystones

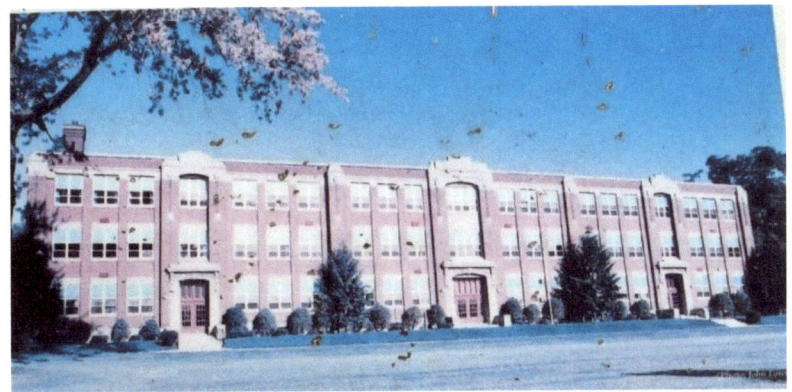

Belleville Collegiate Institute and Vocational School opened
September 1928 on Church Street as the only high school in
Belleville. The school closed its doors to students in 1992 and
stood empty for twelve years before being demolished in 2004.
Neo-gothic (Collegiate Gothic) architecture – three-storey
rectangular brick structure, perimeter of classrooms around a
central core with two gymnasiums on the lower floors and an
ornate 1,000 plus-seat auditorium on the upper floors

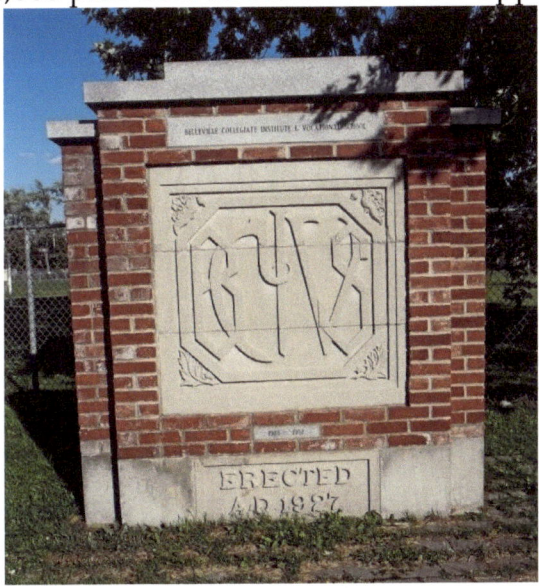

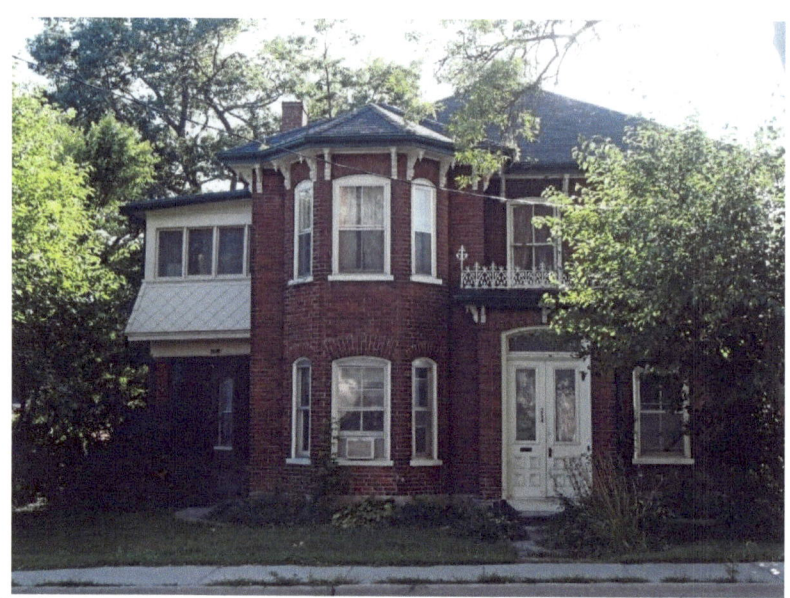

254 Church Street – cornice brackets, two-storey bay window, voussoirs, iron cresting

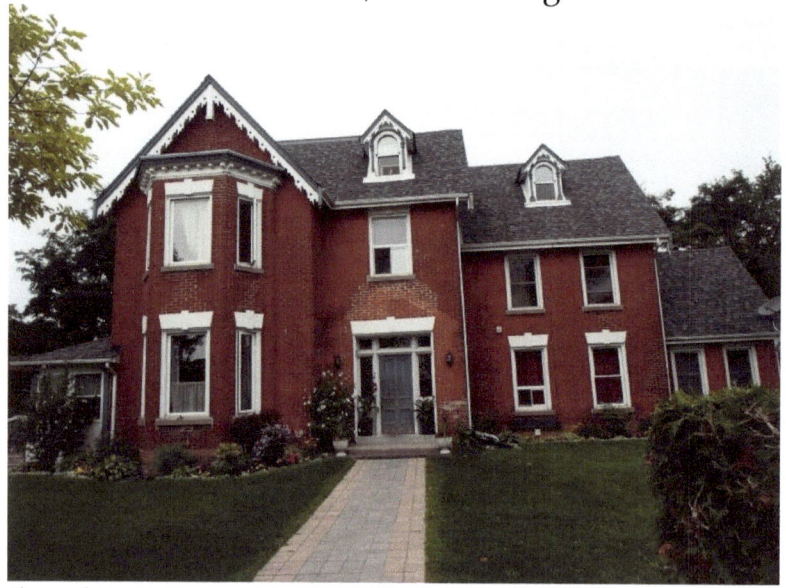

4 Church Street – verge board trim and finial on gable, two-storey bay window, dormers with trim, keystones, sidelights and transom window

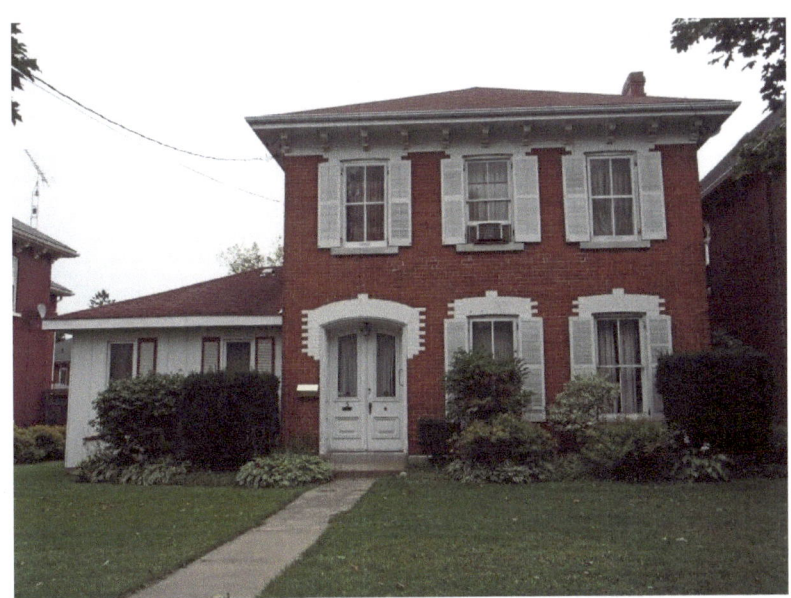

5 Church Street – hipped roof, cornice brackets, voussoirs with keystones

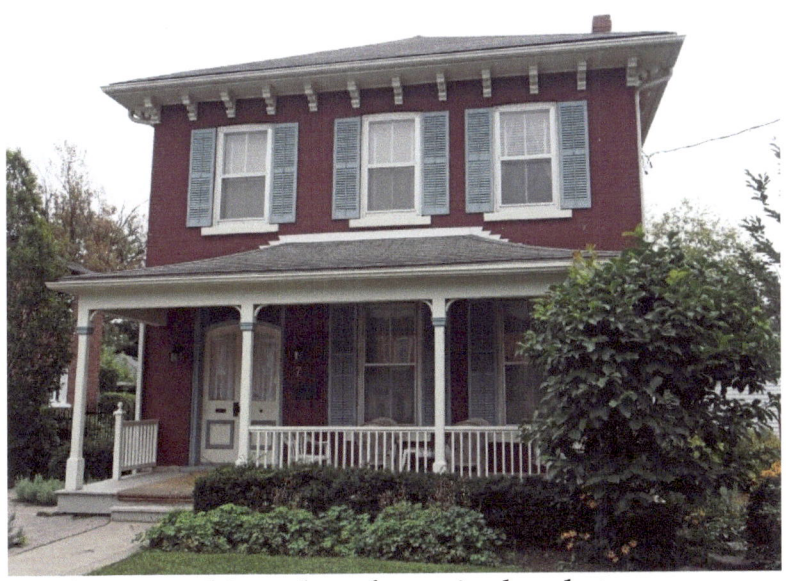

7 Church Street – hipped roof, cornice brackets, open veranda railing

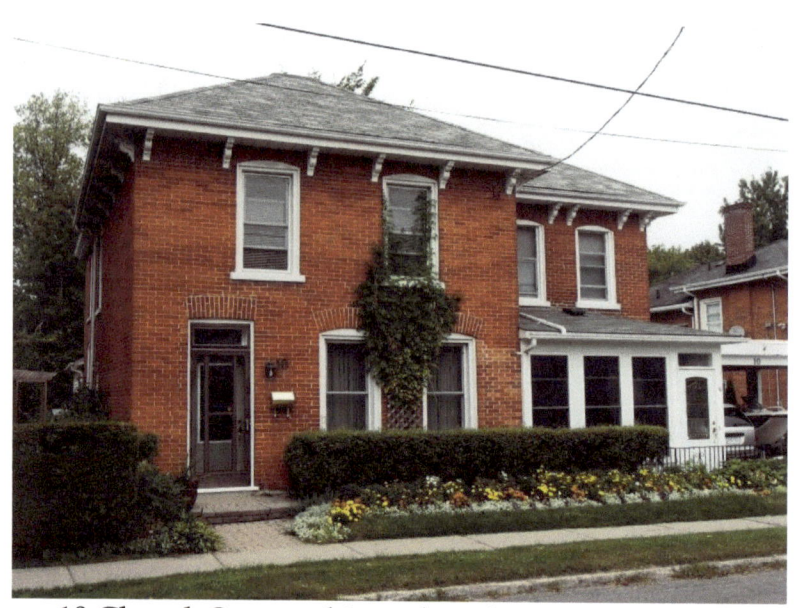

10 Church Street – hipped roof, cornice brackets

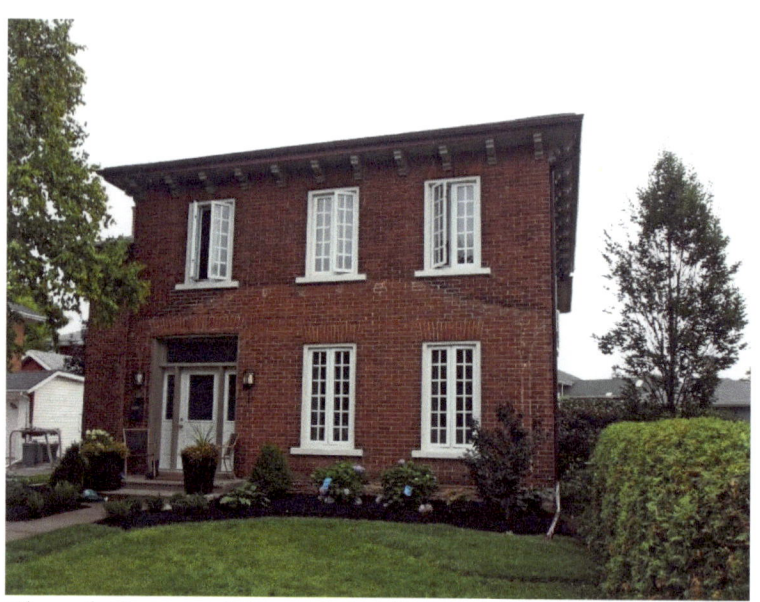

14 Church Street – hipped roof, cornice brackets, sidelights

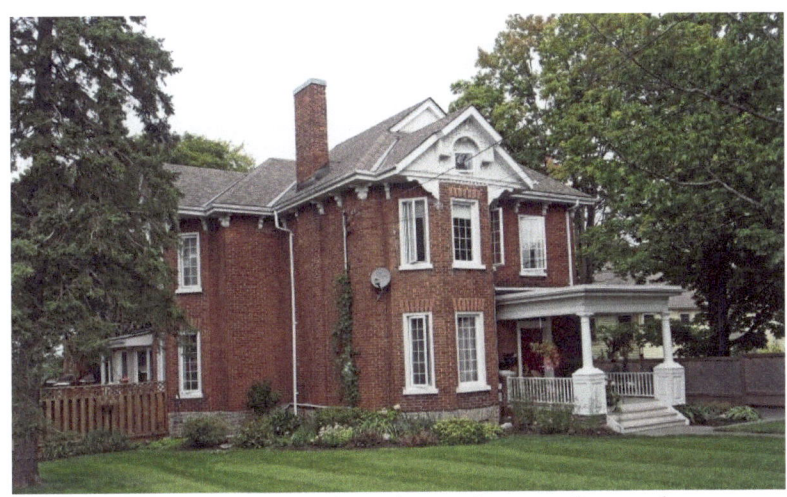

22 Church Street – cornice brackets, fretwork, sunburst pattern in gable

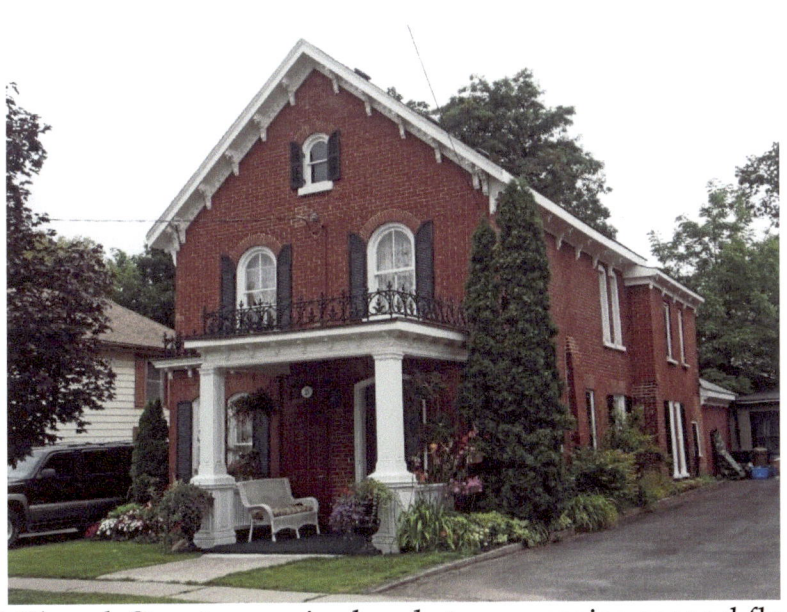

25 Church Street – cornice brackets, voussoirs, second floor balcony

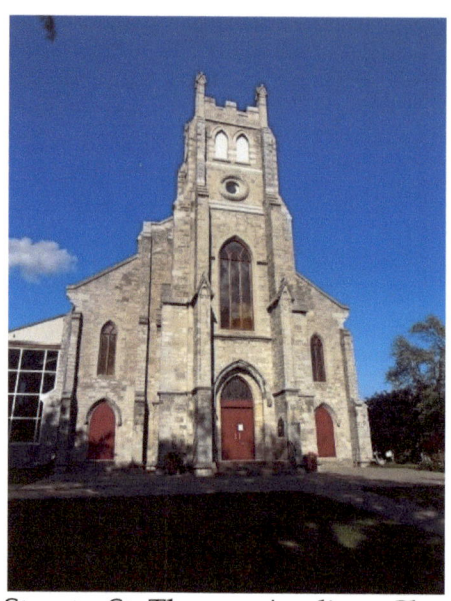

201 Church Street – St. Thomas Anglican Church – 1870s -
Traditional Norman-style (Romanesque) church, joined to a modern
glass-enveloped Parish Centre – rounded windows with muntins,
quoining, buttresses, finials, beveled dentil molding

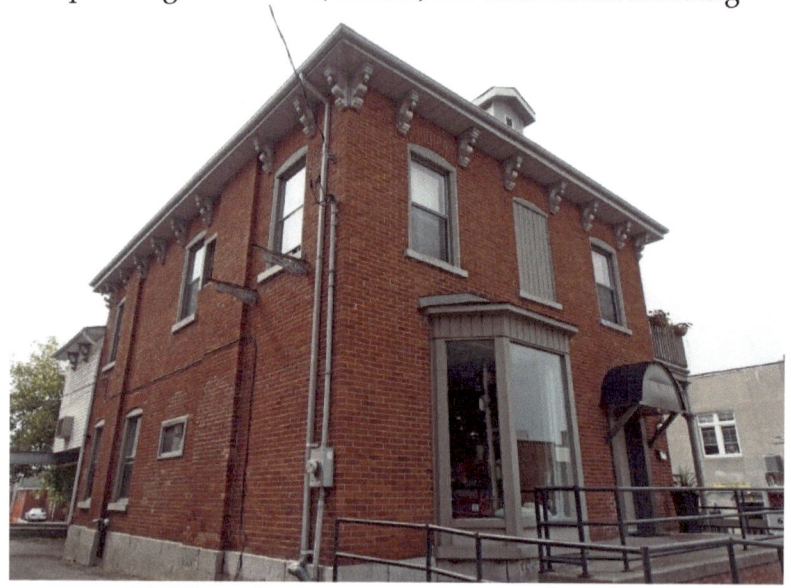

11 Victoria Avenue – cornice brackets

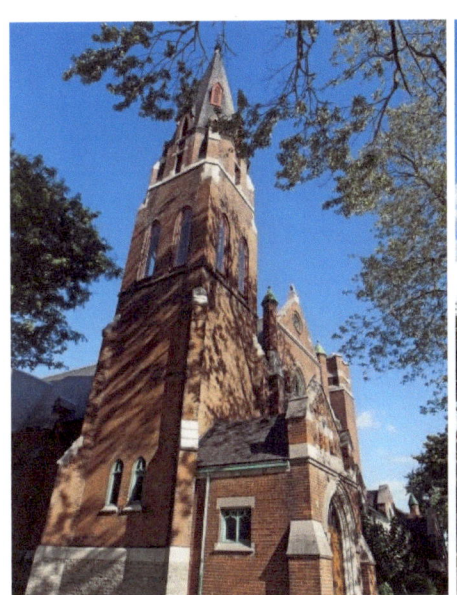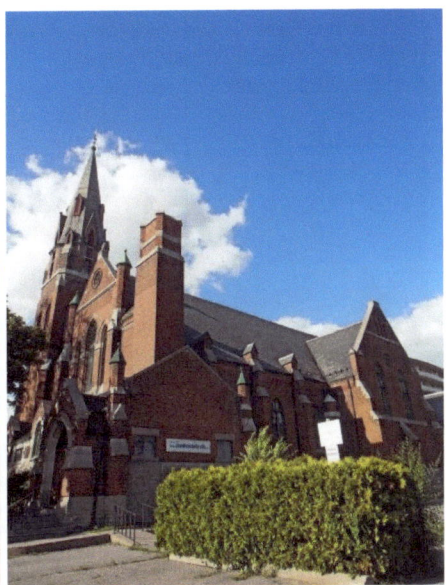

67 Victoria Avenue (corner of Church Street) – St. Andrew's
Presbyterian Church – 1895 – lancet windows with muntins;
buttresses, brick courses, finials, rose window

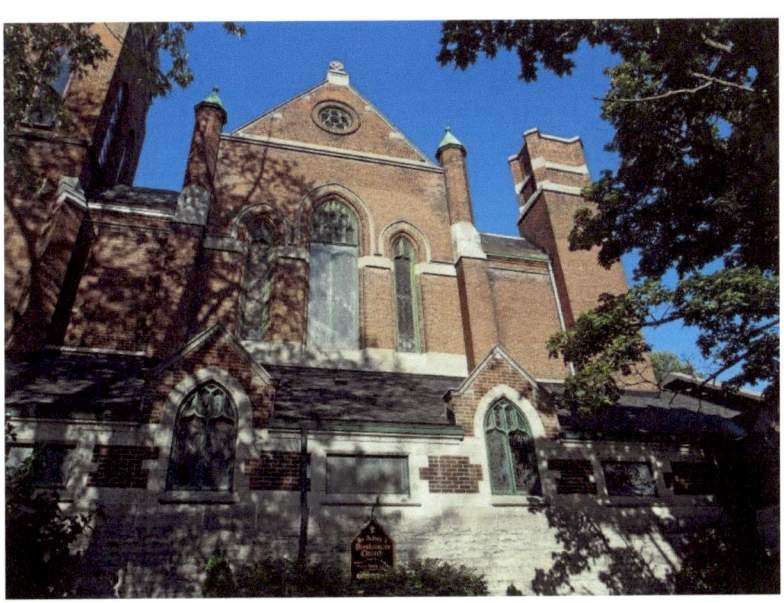

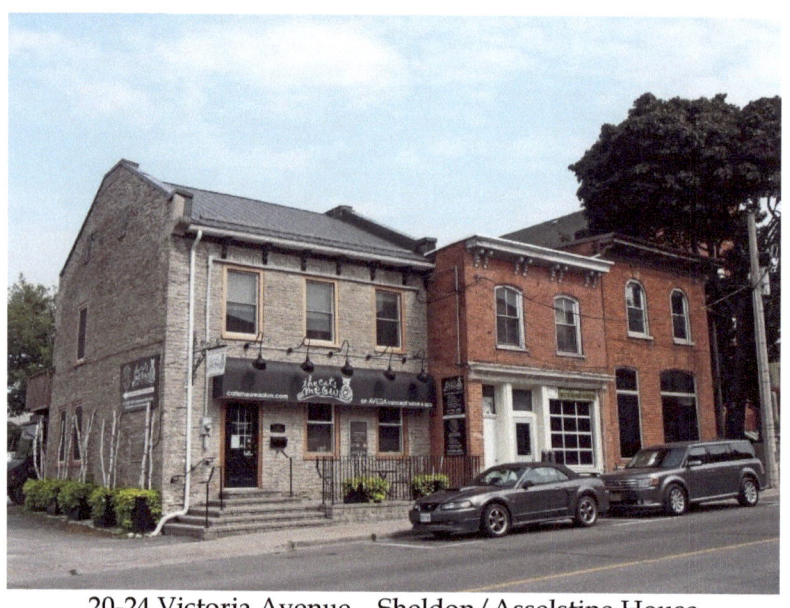

20-24 Victoria Avenue – Sheldon/Asselstine House
20 Victoria – Classical Vernacular – built 1836 - cut limestone facade with balanced arrangement of window and door openings; rubble stone side walls rise to parapets at the roof, supported by carved stone corbels.
24 Victoria – Victorian Commercial – built 1879 - second floor has two sash windows and cornice brackets – Asselstine sold pianos and organs

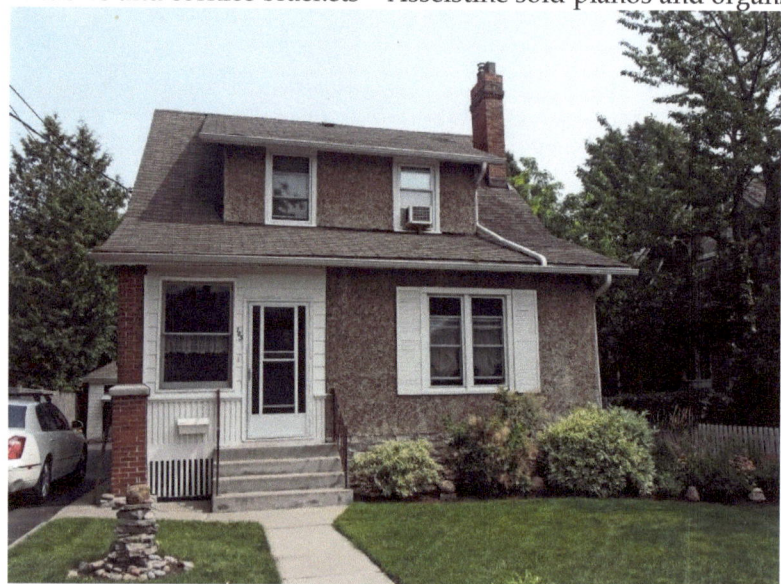

185 John Street – shed dormer

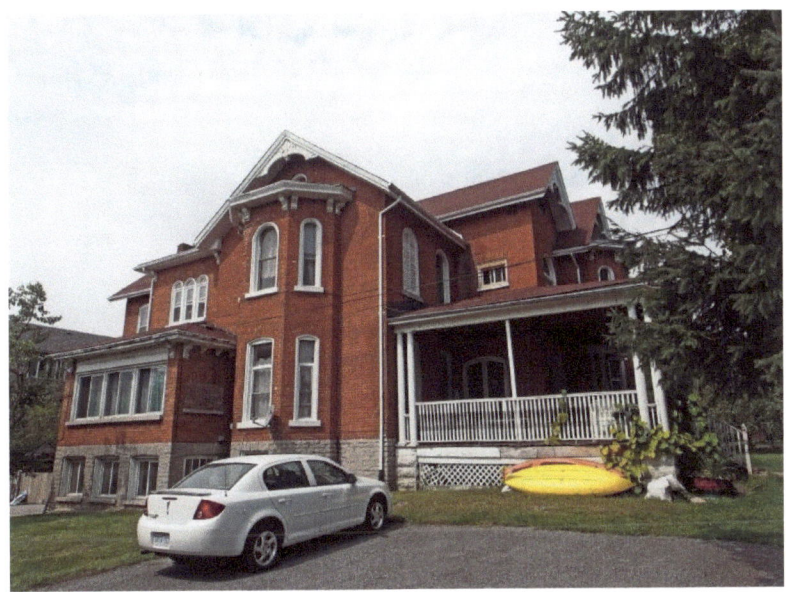

John Street – Queen Anne style – varied roof lines, two-storey
bay window, cornice brackets, verge board trim on gable

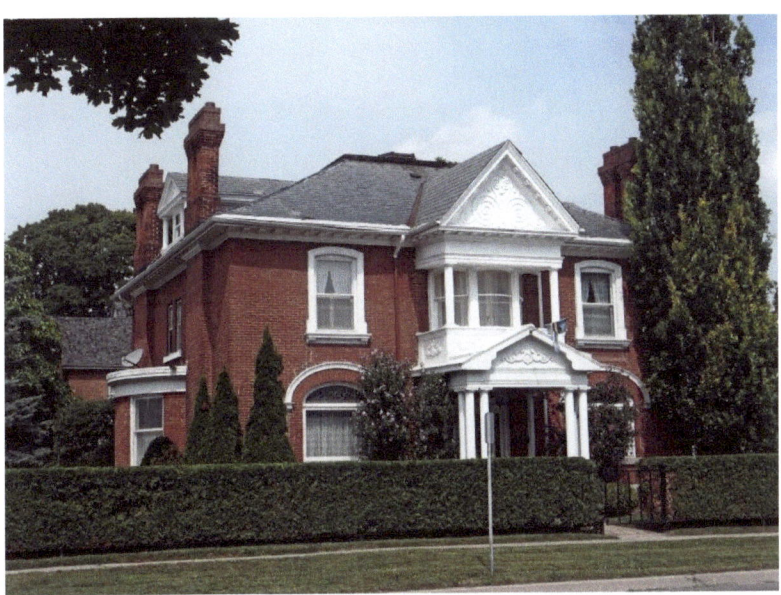

John Street – hipped roof, dormer, tall chimneys, pediments
with decorated tympanums, bay window on side

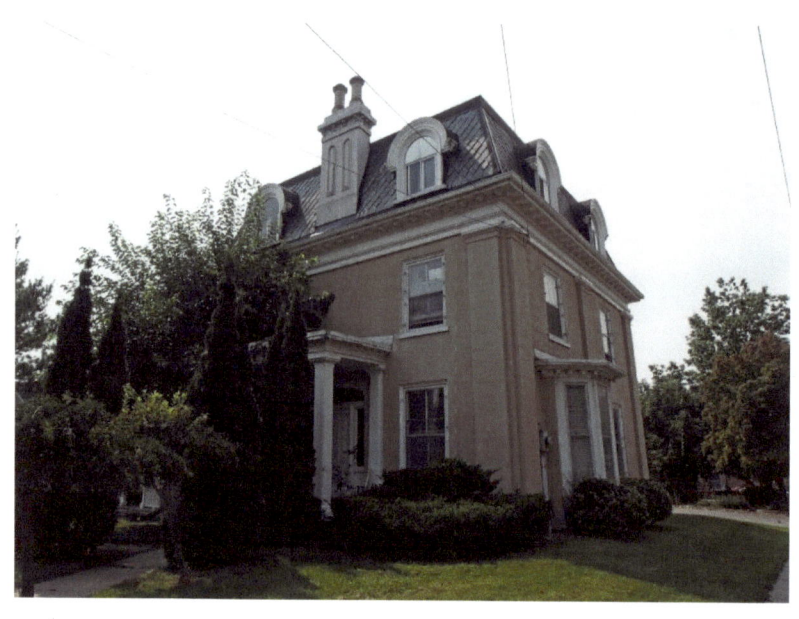

200 John Street – Second Empire style – mansard roof, dormers with window hoods, tall chimneys, bay window

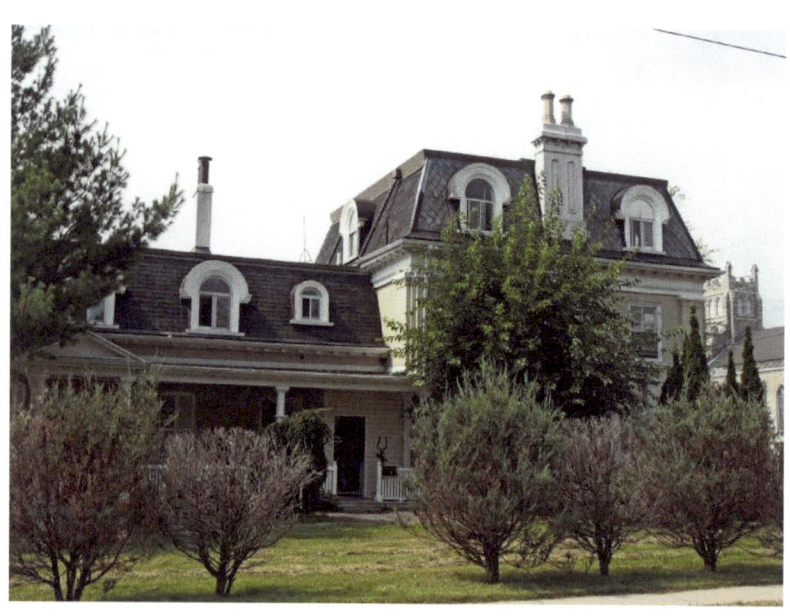

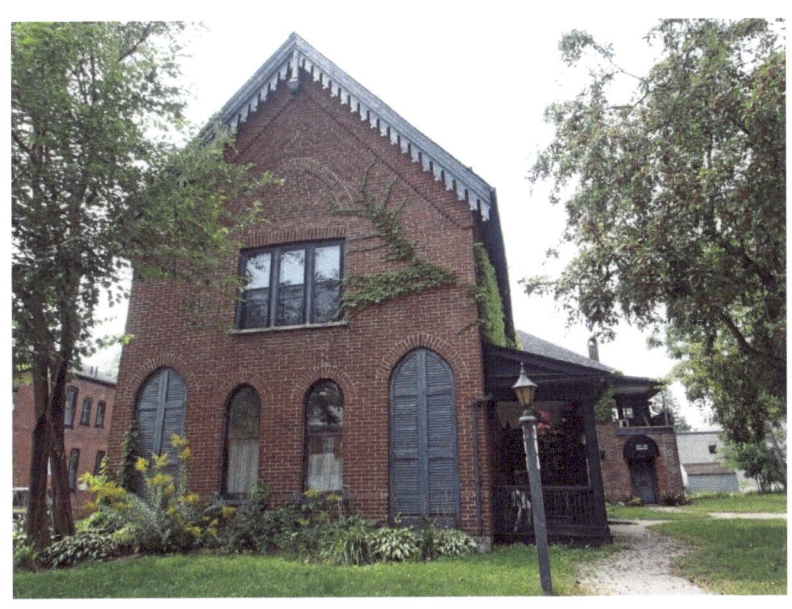

208 John Street – verge board trim and finial on gable

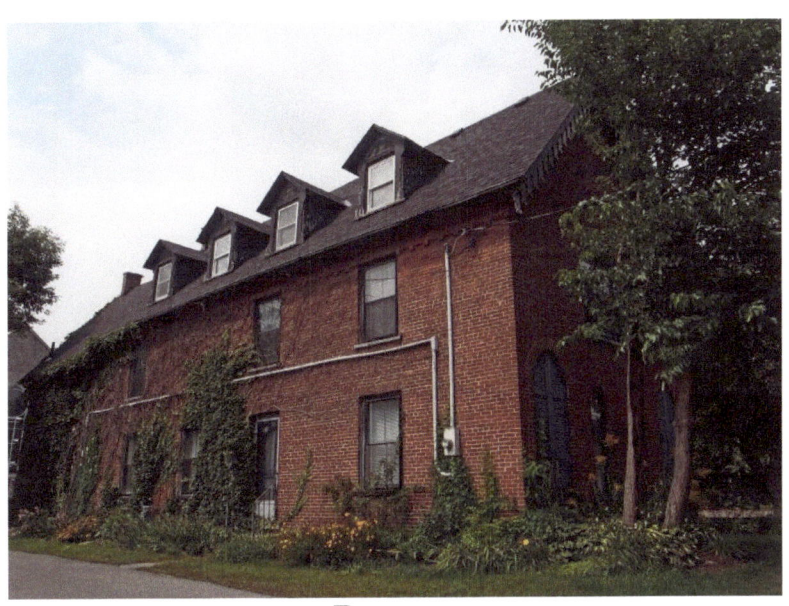

Dormers

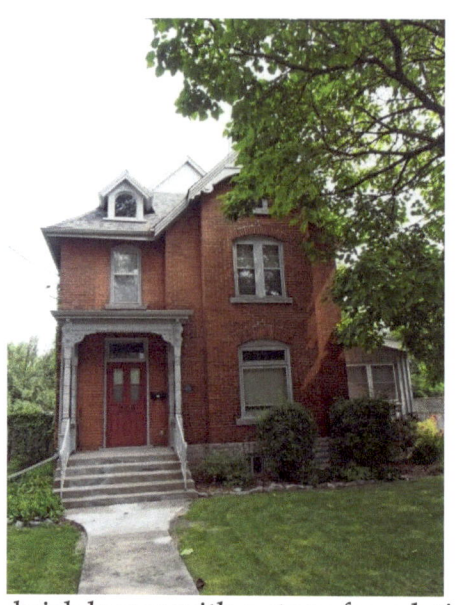

209 John Street – brick house with a stone foundation, dormer, 2½-storey frontispiece with verge board trim on gable; small porch with decorative jagged wooden sheathing around a flat roof, supported by four pillars

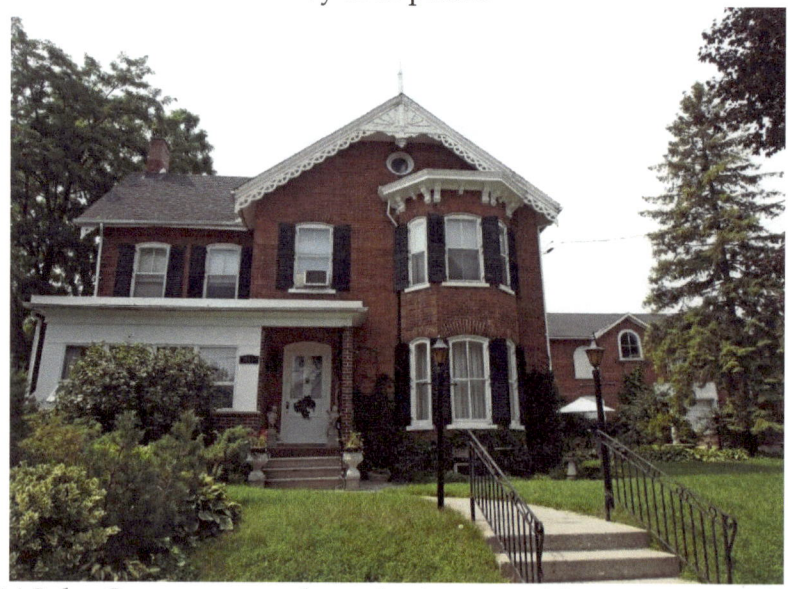

214 John Street - verge board trim on gable, two-storey bay window with cornice brackets

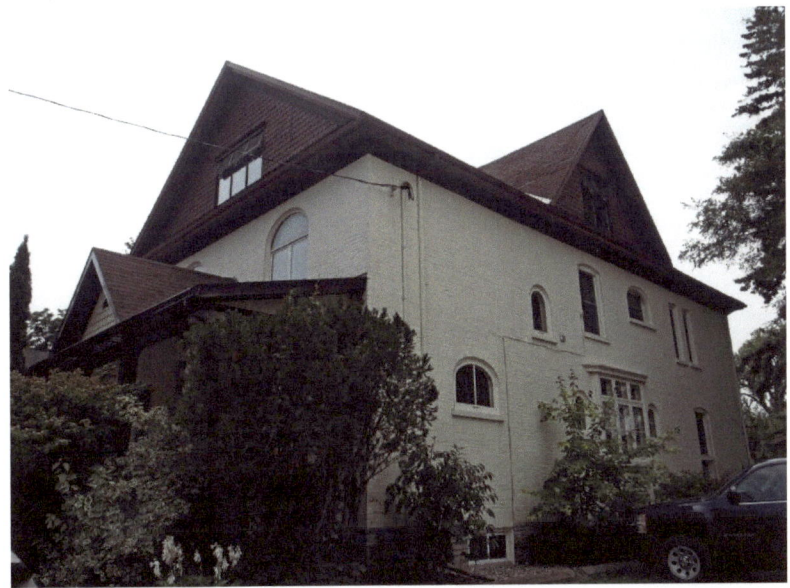

220 John Street

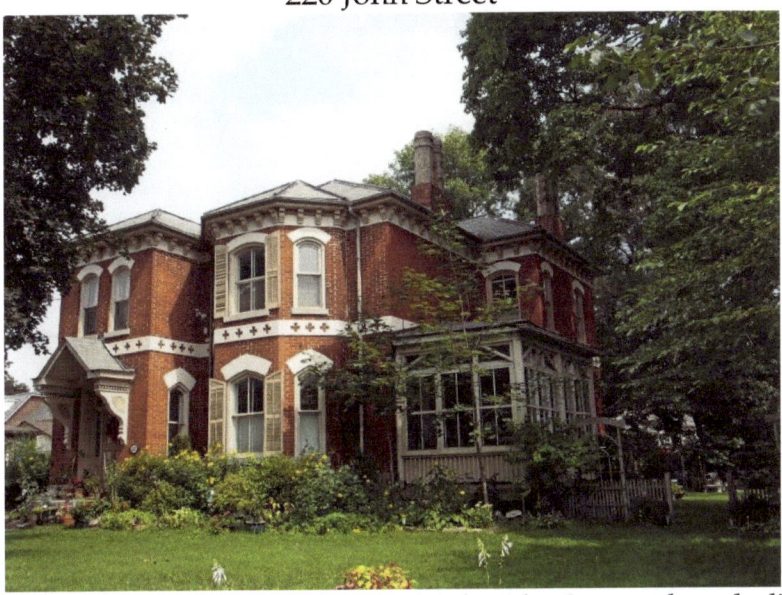

221 John Street – Built 1871, two-storey brick with a 2-storey bay; the lintels are off-white brick and match the decorative course surrounding the house at the second floor level; chimneys are Tudor type with brick bases topped with small string courses; front porch has wooden gable roof supported by massive wooden brackets, **cornice brackets under eaves**

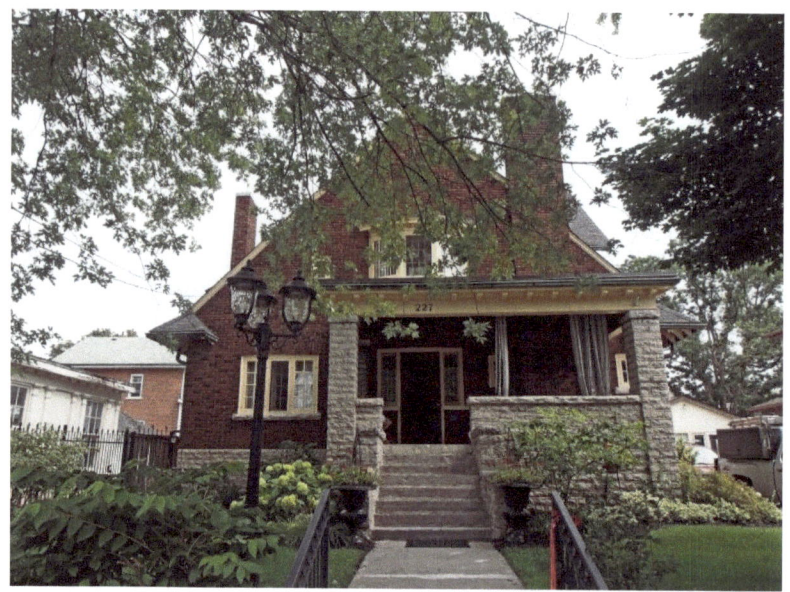

227 John Street – bay window above veranda – heritage property

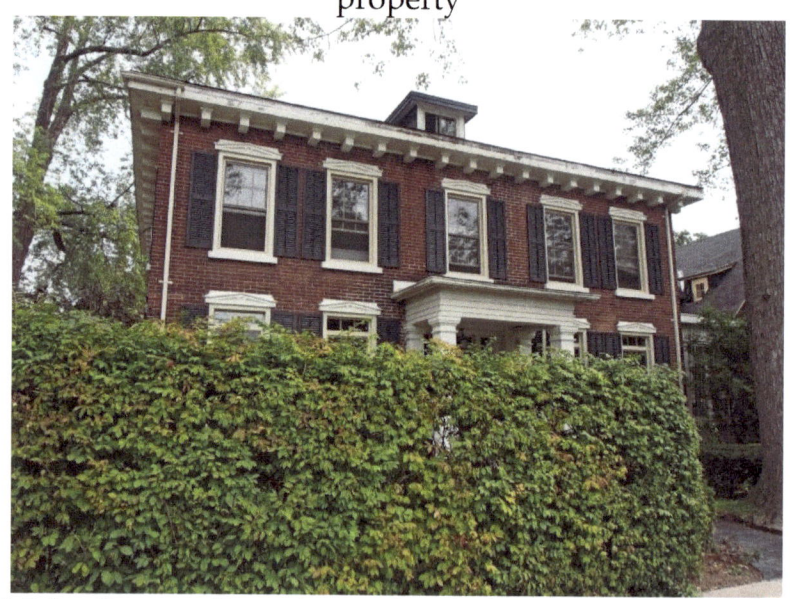

231 John Street – Georgian style – balanced façade, dormer – heritage property

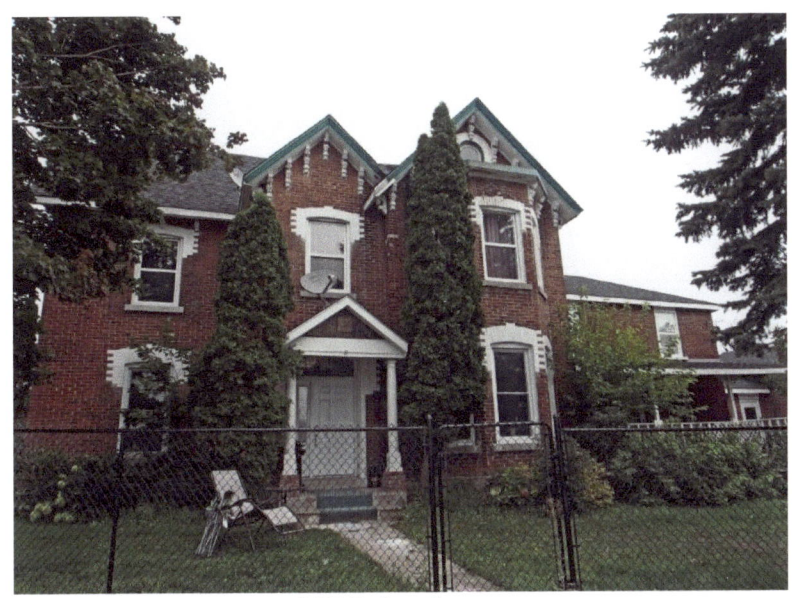

295 John Street

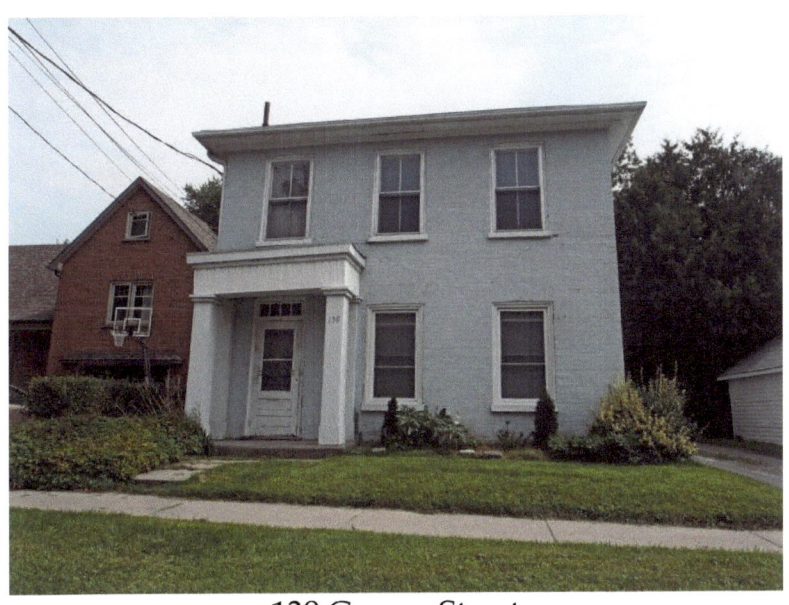

139 George Street

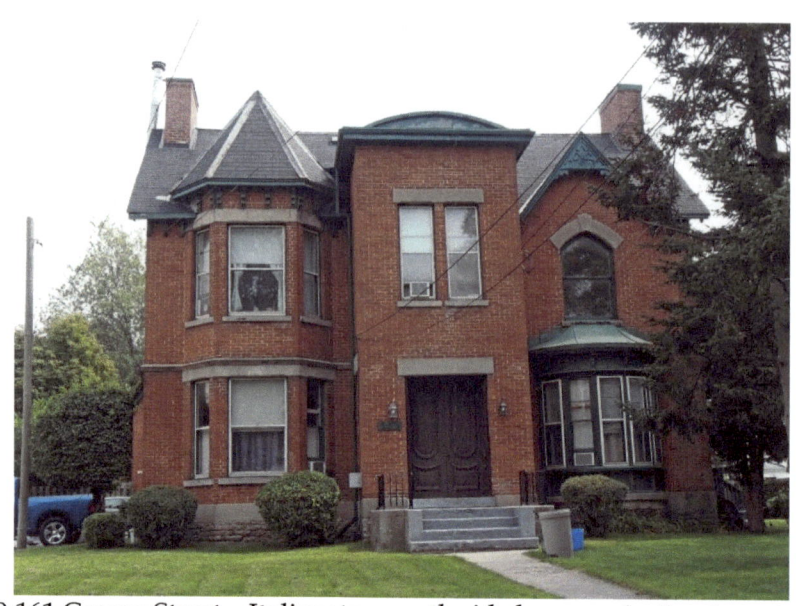

159-161 George Street – Italianate – north side has a projecting two storey bay with a string course above the ground floor windows; south side has a projecting five window bay with carved wood paneling above it; window above has an arched lintel, two-storey frontispiece, gable with verge board trim – heritage property

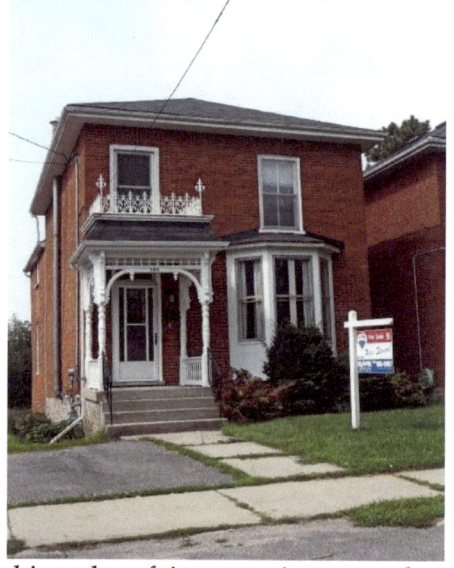

168 George Street – hipped roof, iron cresting around second floor balcony, bay window

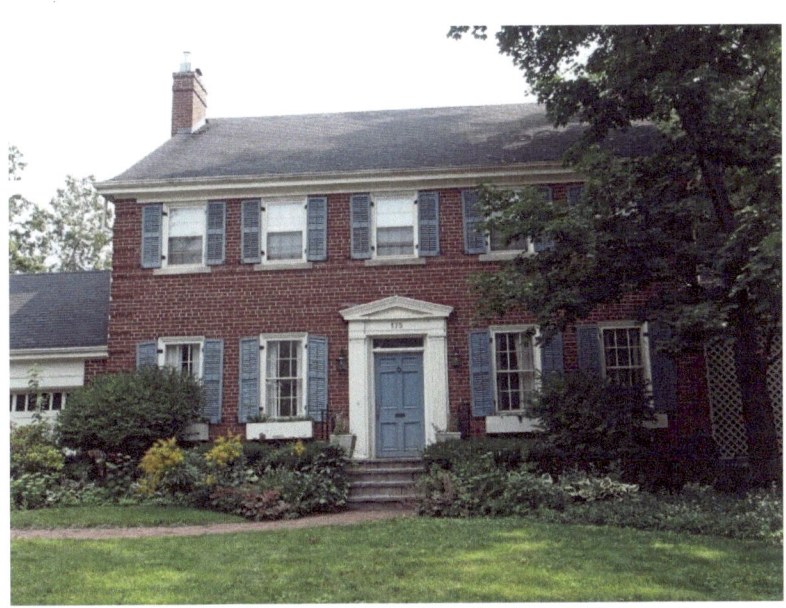

175 George Street – Georgian style – balanced façade, engaged columns surrounding door with pediment above, transom window

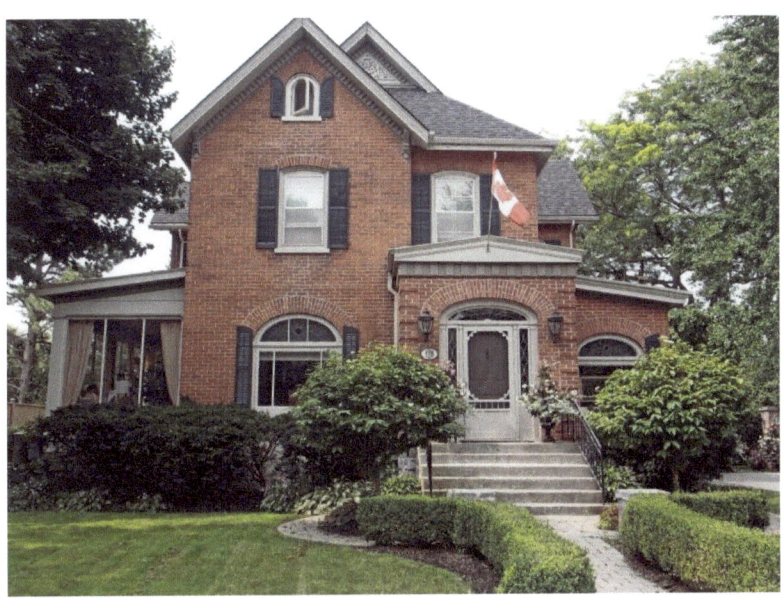

178 George Street

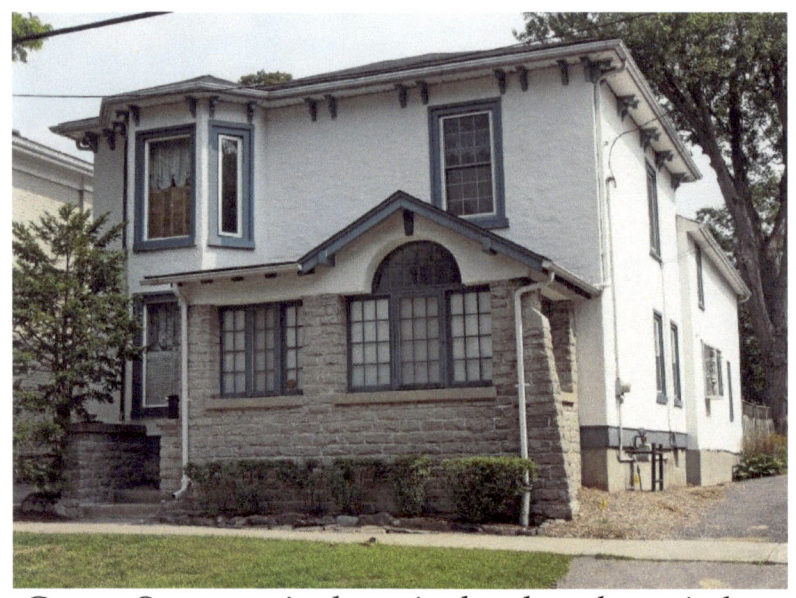

George Street – paired cornice brackets, bay window

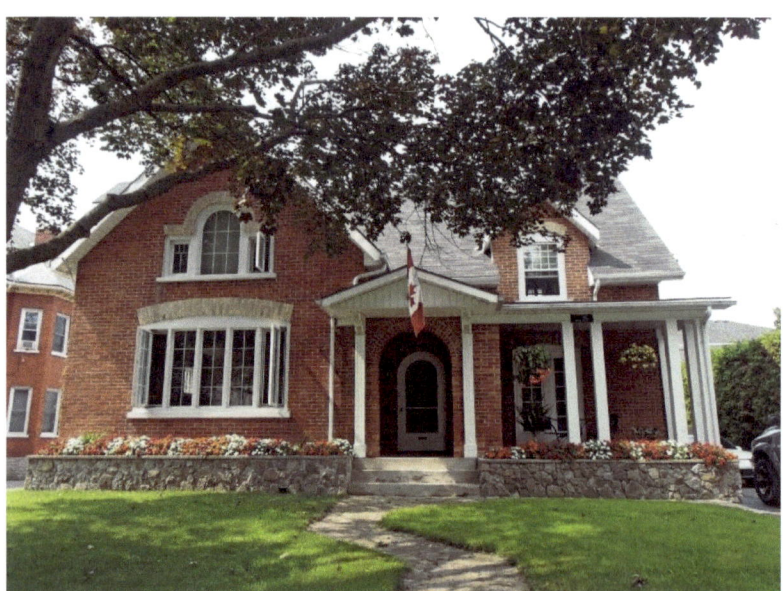

192 George Street – dichromatic voussoirs, Palladian-type window

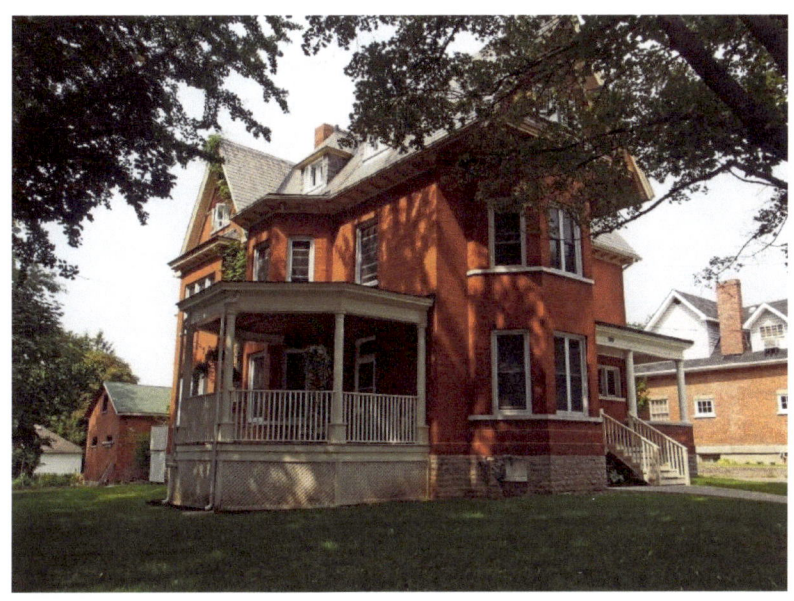

190 George Street – 2½-storey tower-like bay window capped with a gable

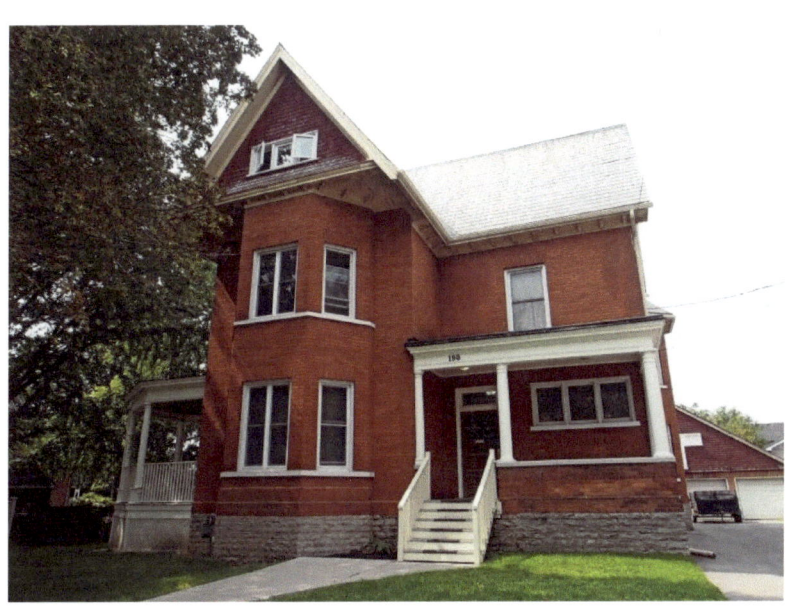

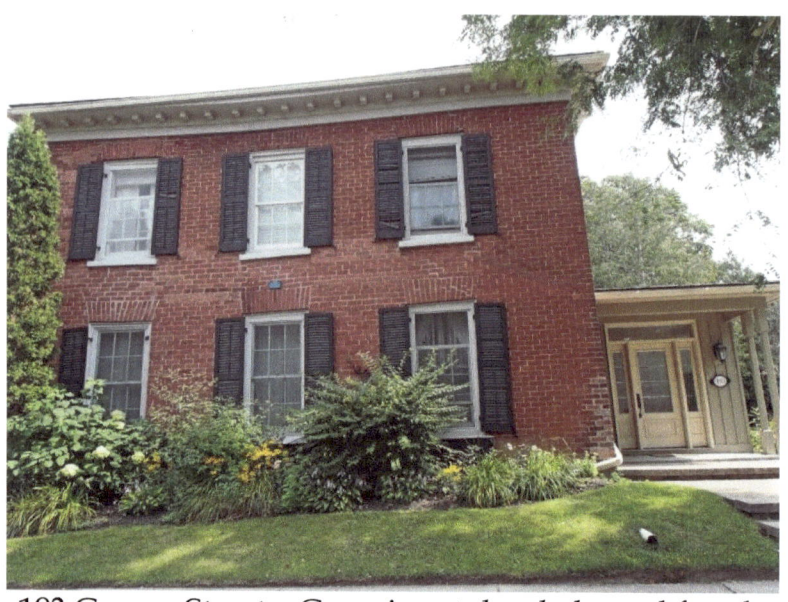

193 George Street – Georgian style – balanced façade
– heritage property

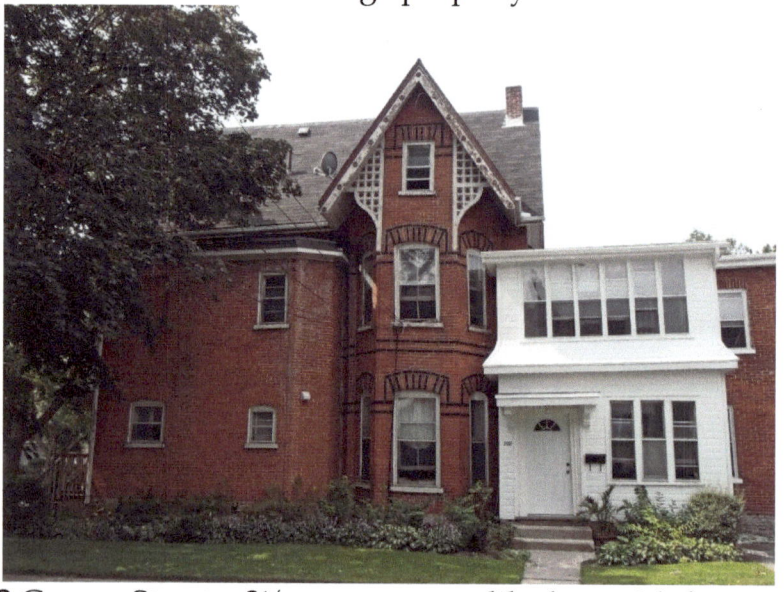

202 George Street – 2½-storey tower-like bay with fretwork,
dichromatic brickwork and banding

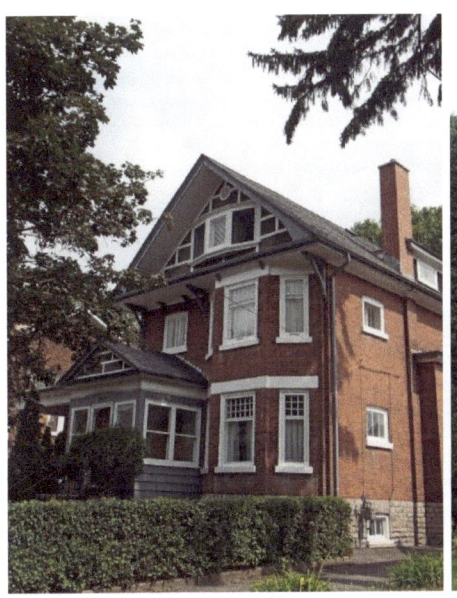

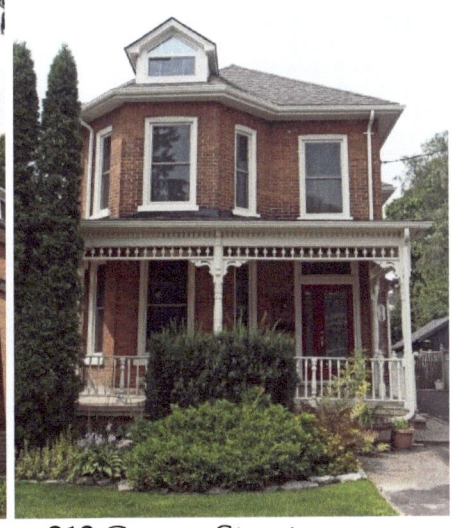

211 George Street
Gabled roof

212 George Street
hipped roof, dormer
Verandah support posts with
decorative capitals and spindles

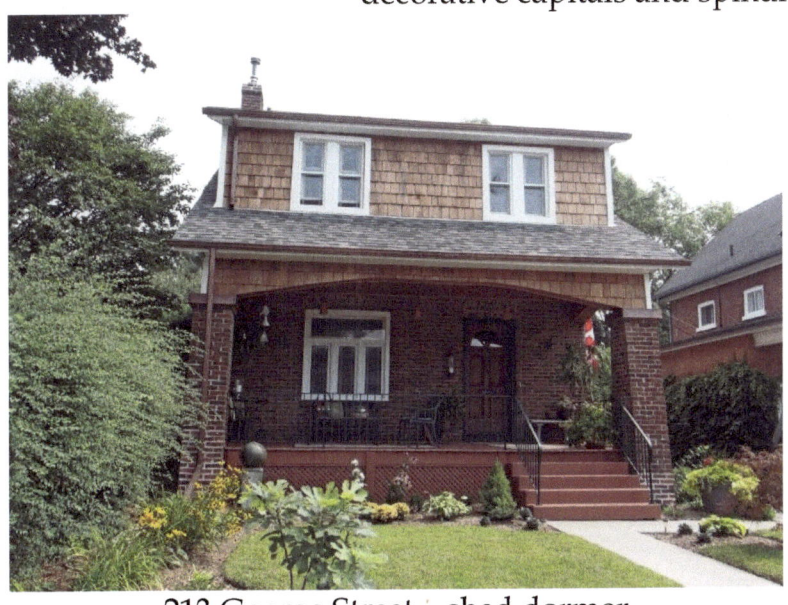

213 George Street – shed dormer

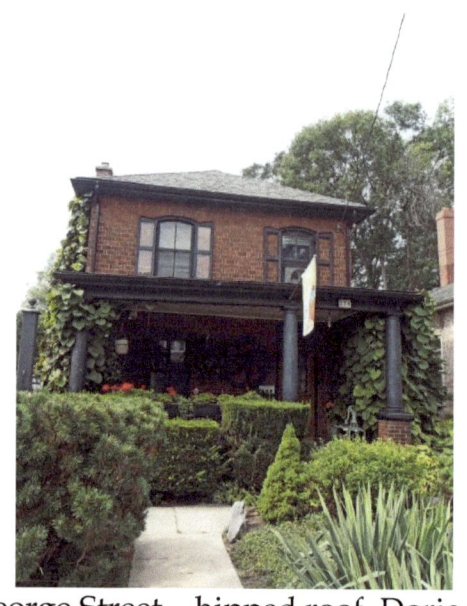

214 George Street – hipped roof, Doric pillars

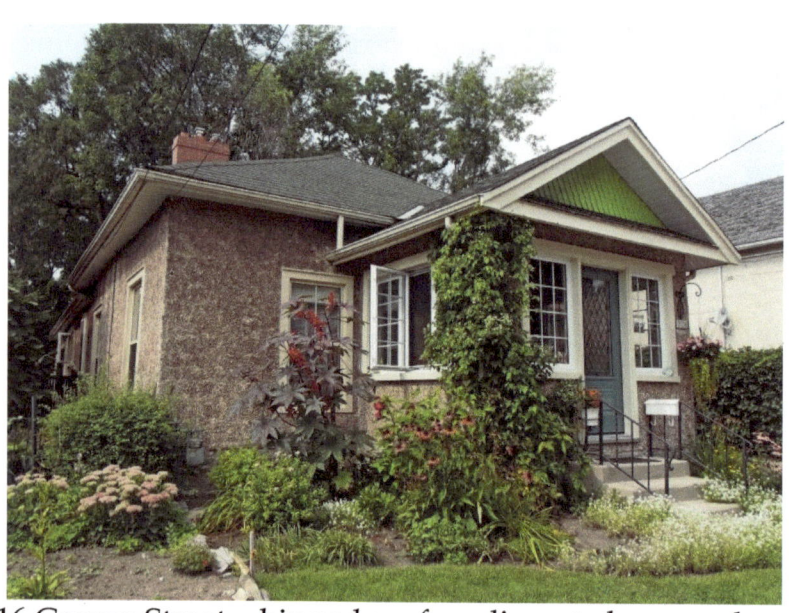

216 George Street – hipped roof, pediment above enclosed porch

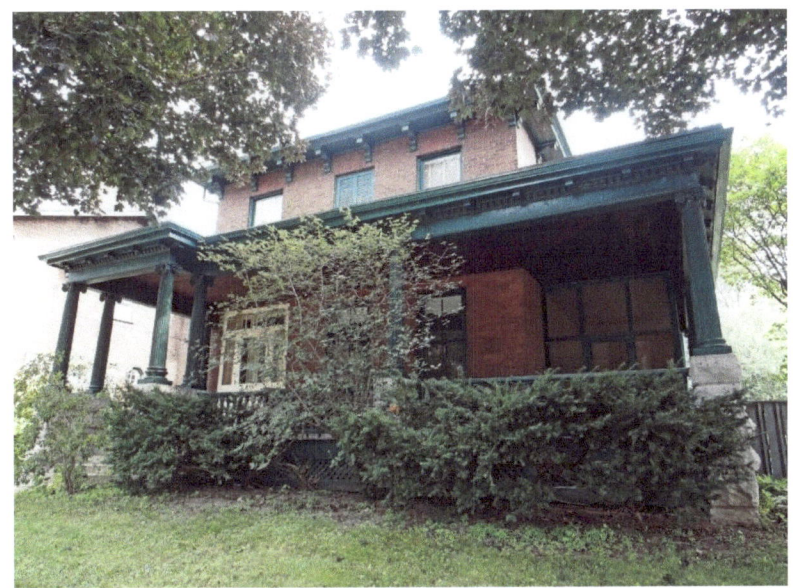

219 George Street – cornice brackets, Ionic capitals on verandah pillars

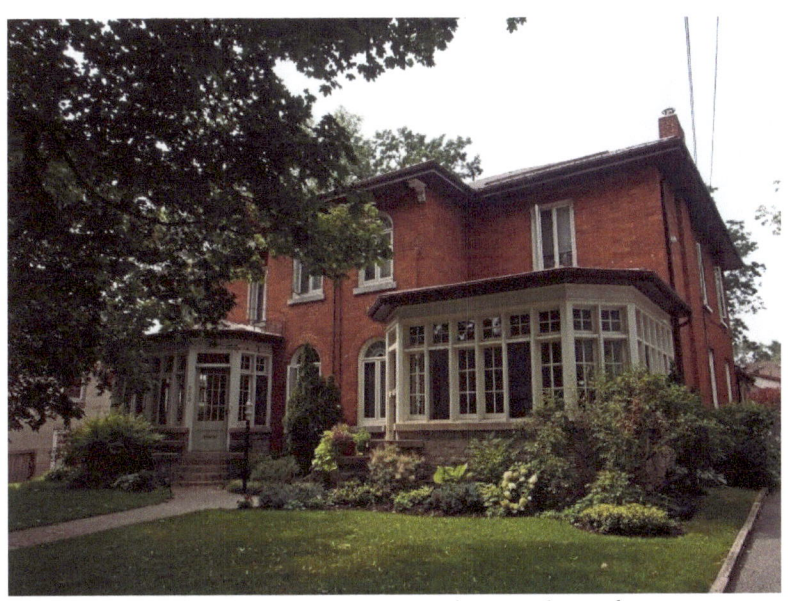

220 George Street – hipped roof

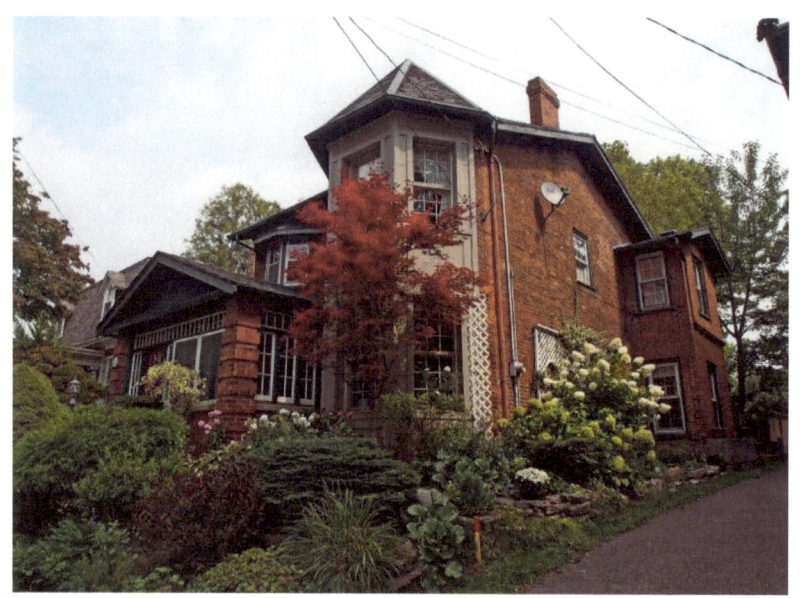

221 George Street – two-storey tower-like bay with cone-shaped roof, pediment

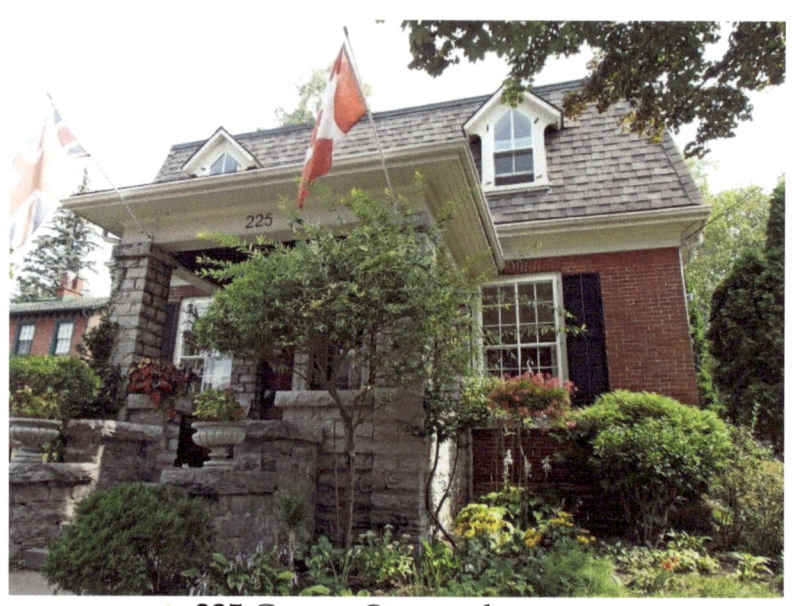

225 George Street - dormers

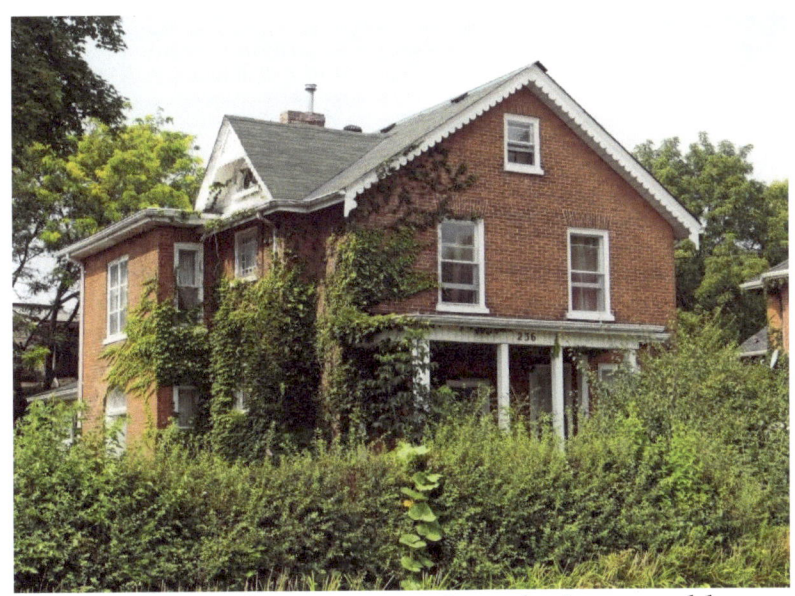

236 George Street – verge board trim on gable

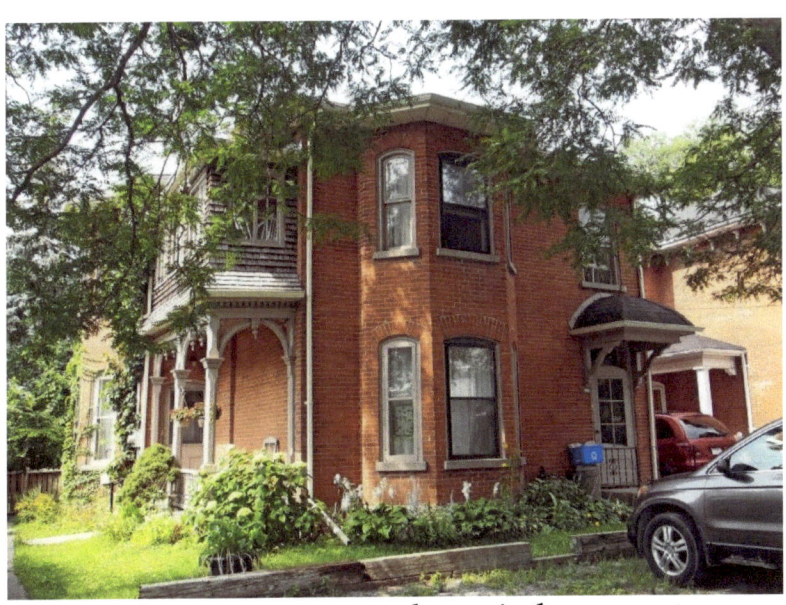

242 George Street – two-storey bay window, ornate veranda supports

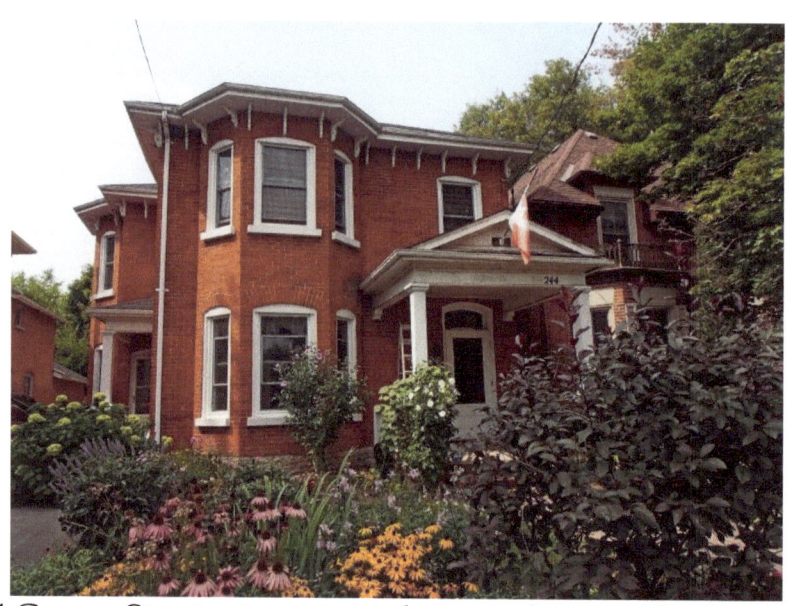

244 George Street – two-storey bay window, cornice brackets, pediment

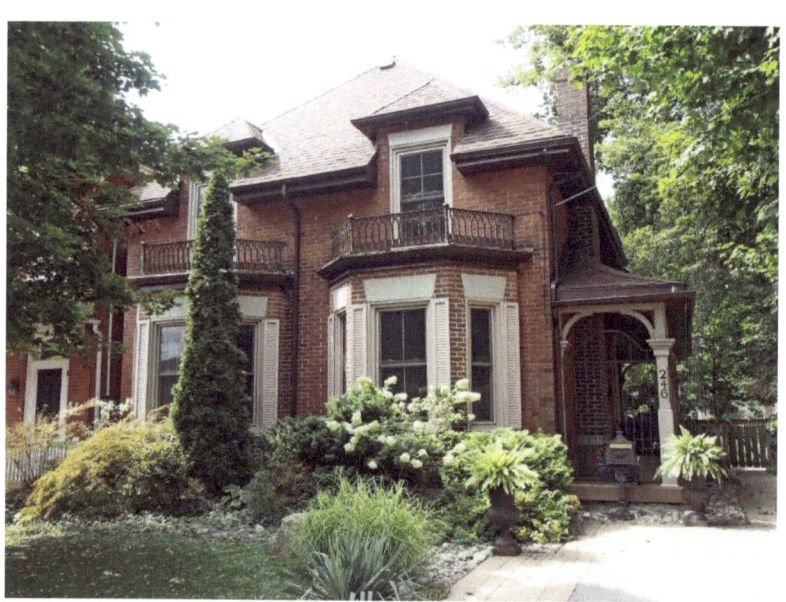

246 George Street – second floor balconies with decorative railings above bay windows

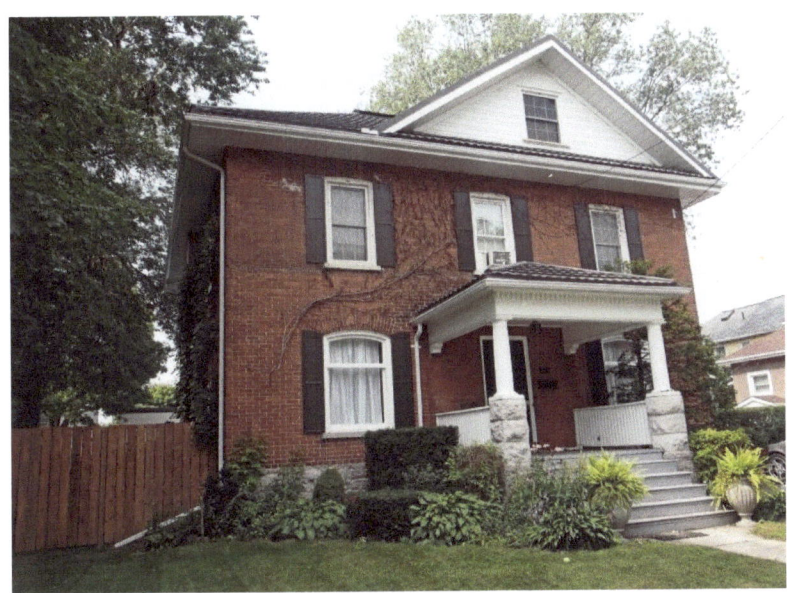

250 George Street – hipped roof with dormer

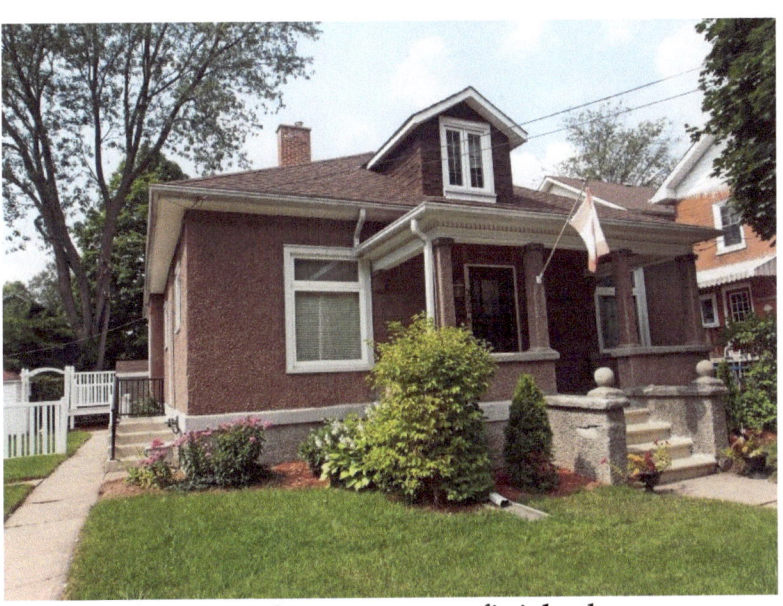

252 George Street – stucco finish, dormer

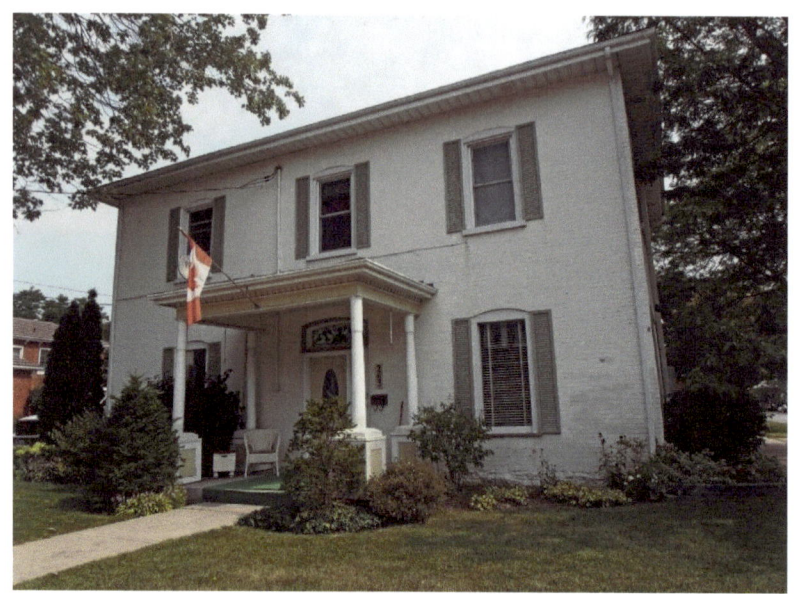

263 George Street

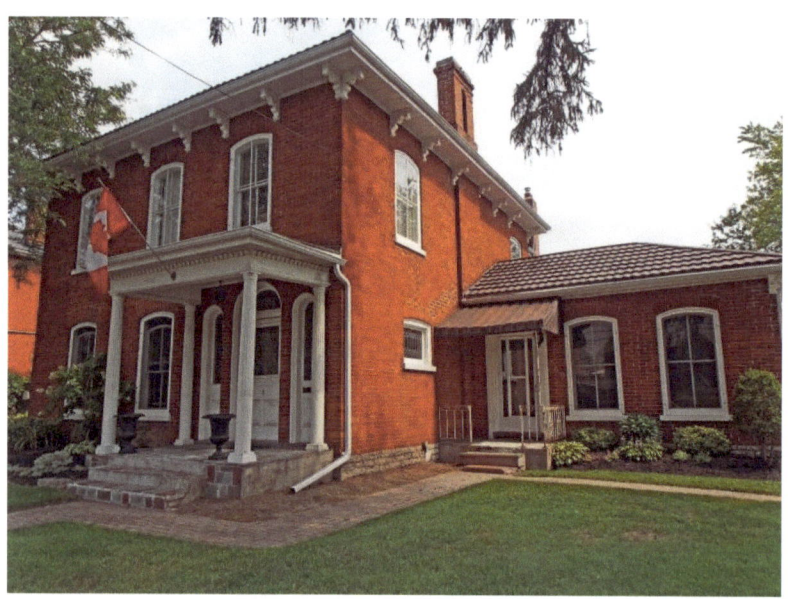

269 George Street – hipped roof, cornice brackets, Doric pillars supporting porch roof

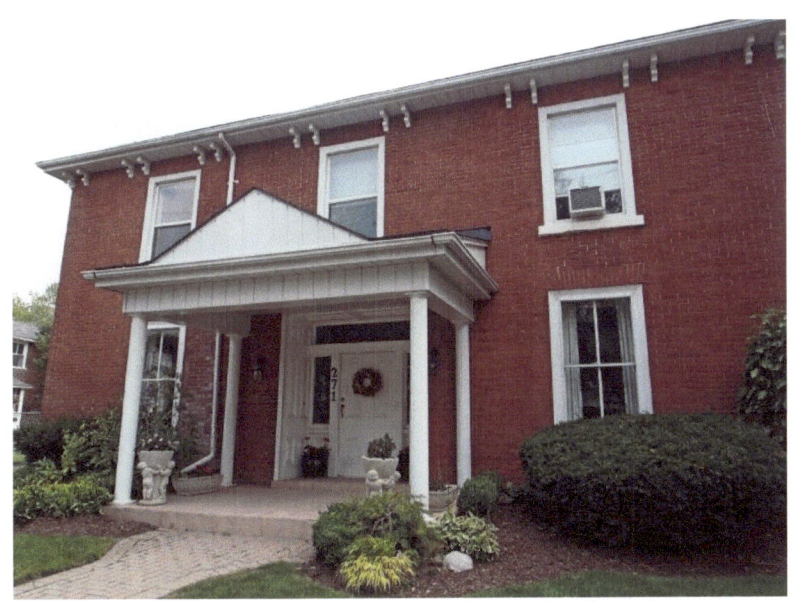

271 George Street – paired cornice brackets

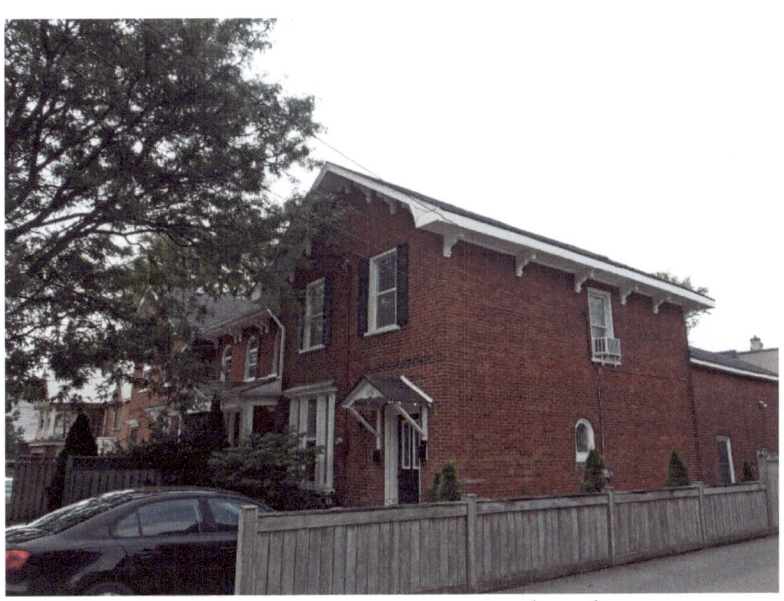

276 George Street – cornice brackets

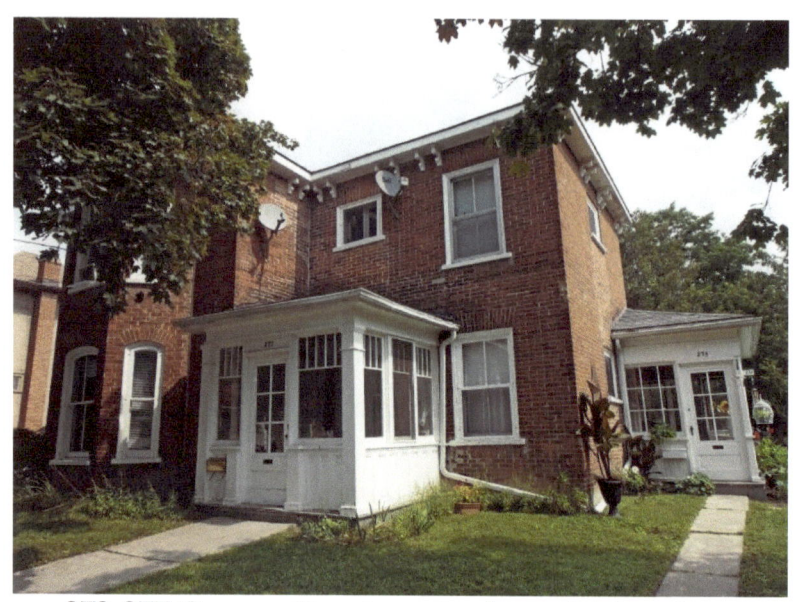

273-277 George Street – paired cornice brackets

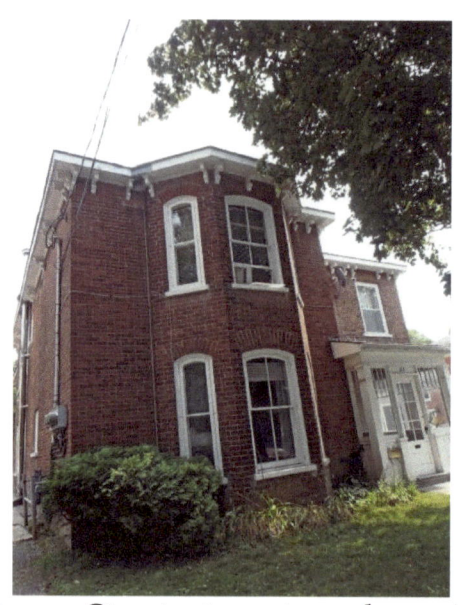

277 George Street – two-storey bay window

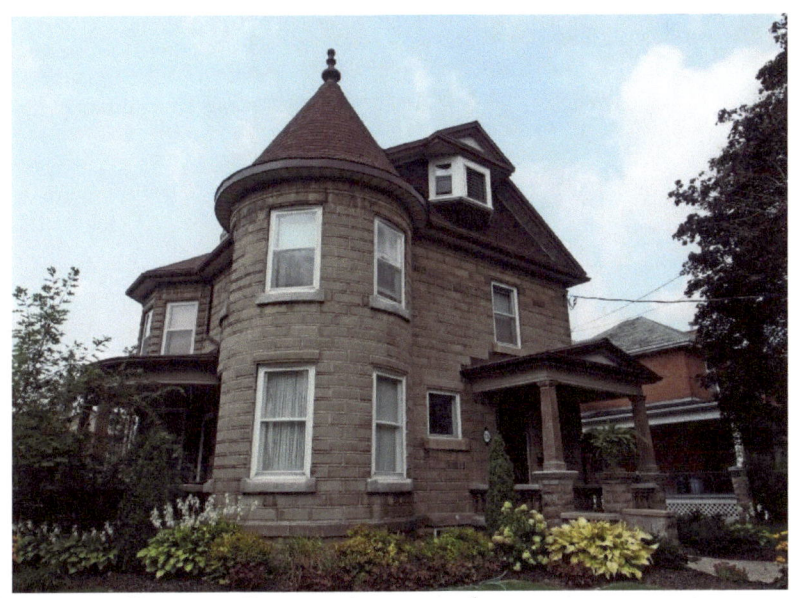

278 George Street – Queen Anne style – two-storey tower with cone-shaped roof, pediment above porch, semi-circular veranda

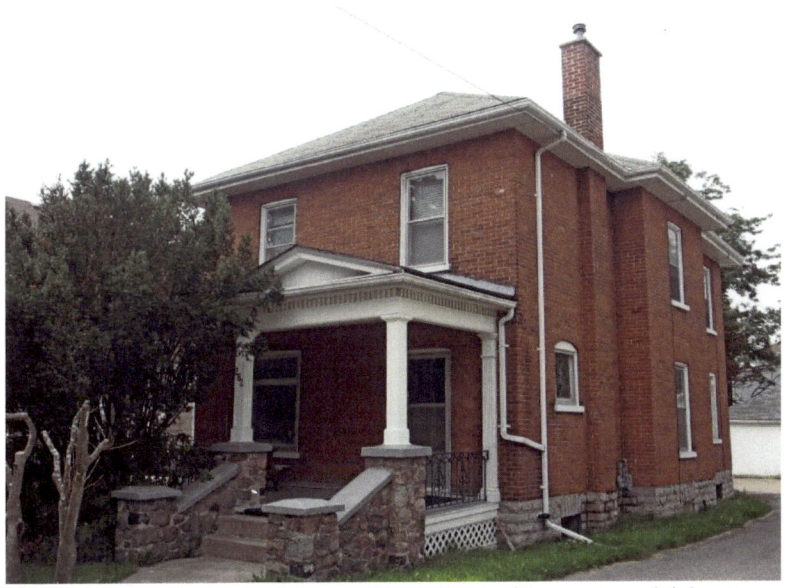

282 George Street – hipped roof, pediment, cobblestone veranda piers

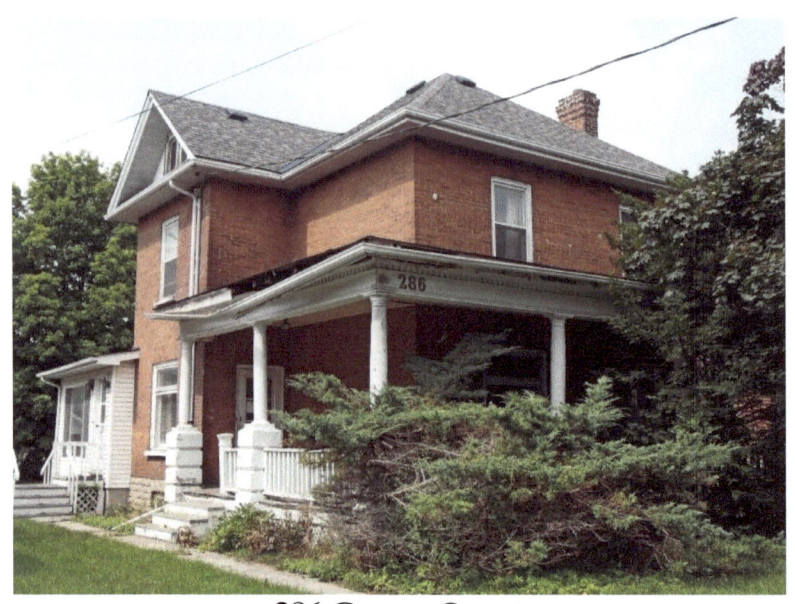

286 George Street

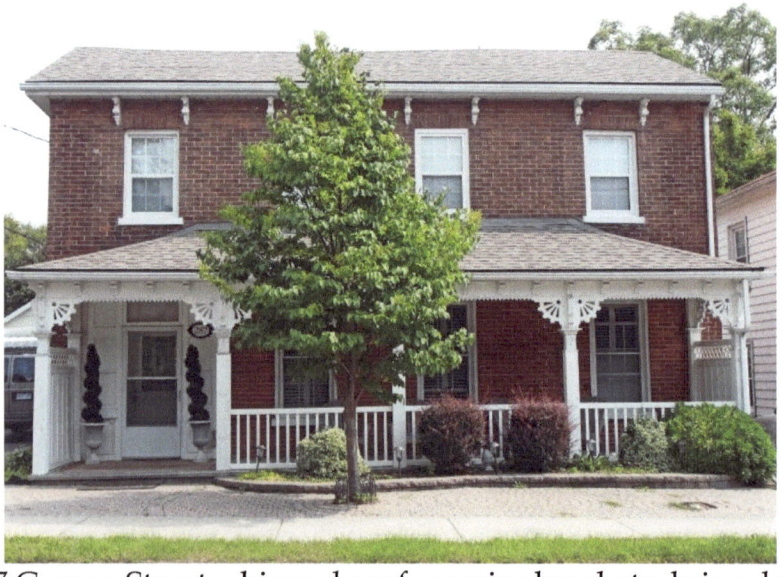

287 George Street – hipped roof, cornice brackets, bric-a-brac on veranda roof supports

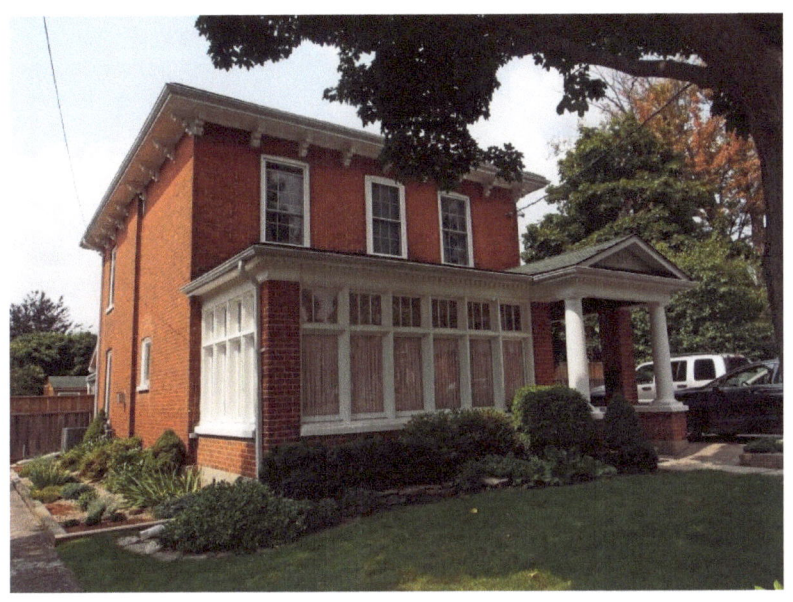

294 George Street – hipped roof, cornice brackets, pediment, Doric pillars

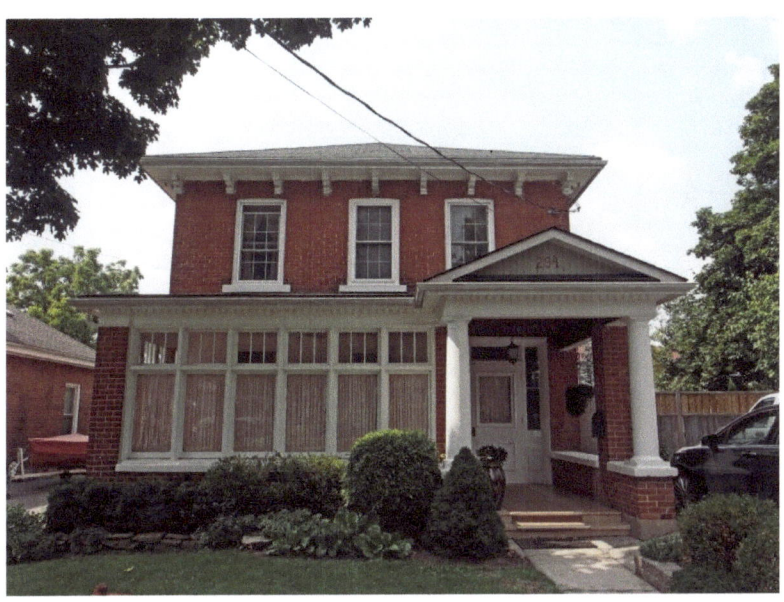

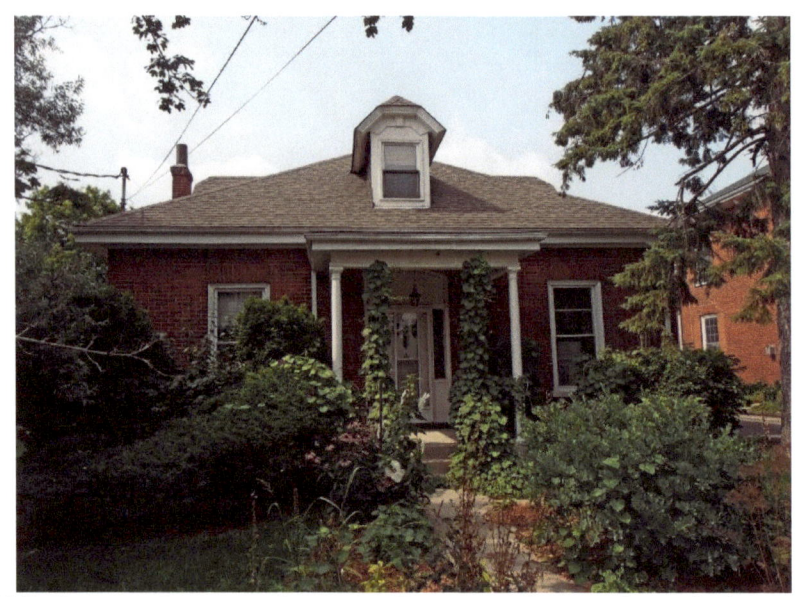

290 George Street – Ontario Cottage - hipped roof, dormer
– heritage property

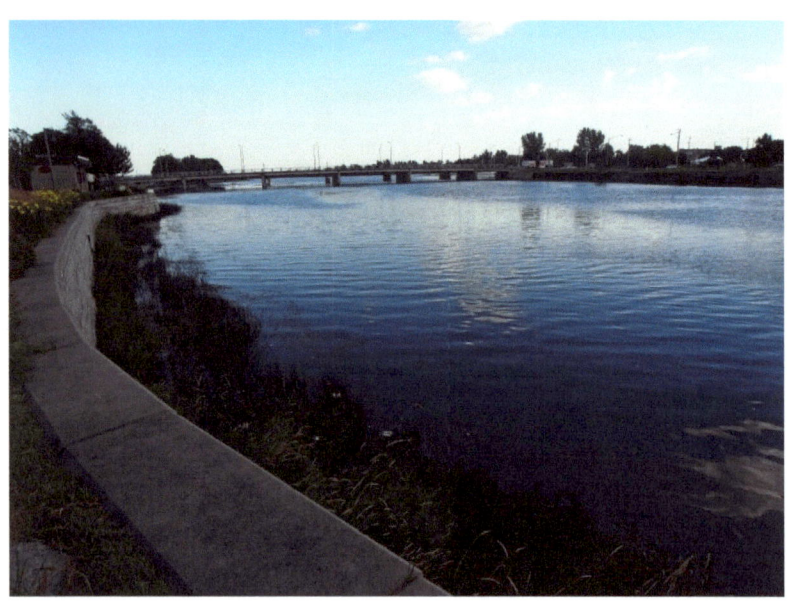

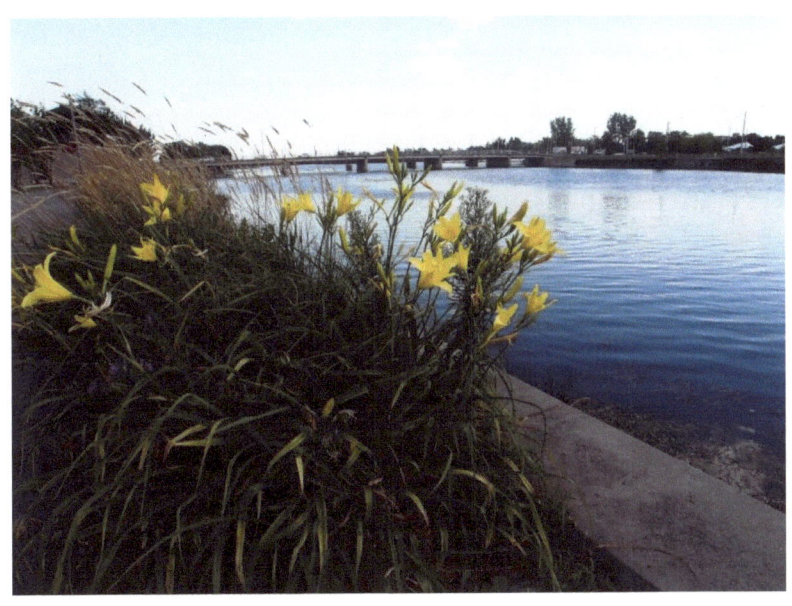

Moira River

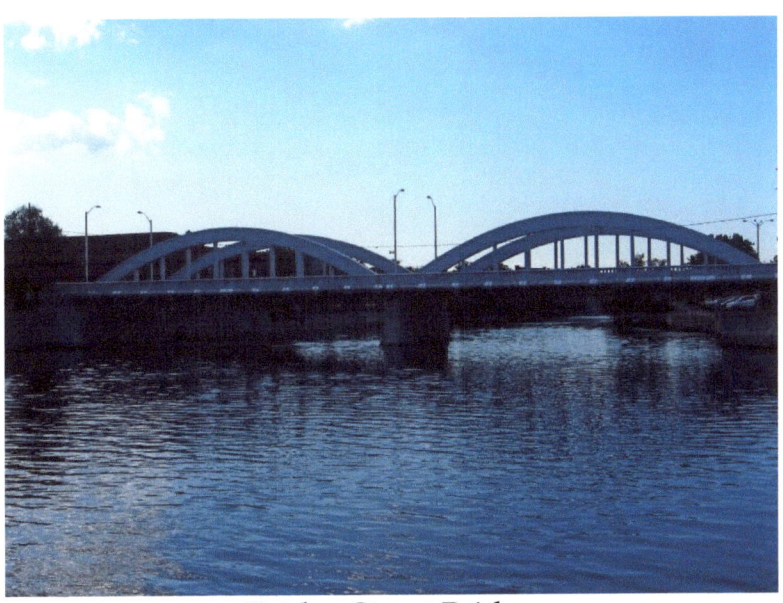

Bridge Street Bridge

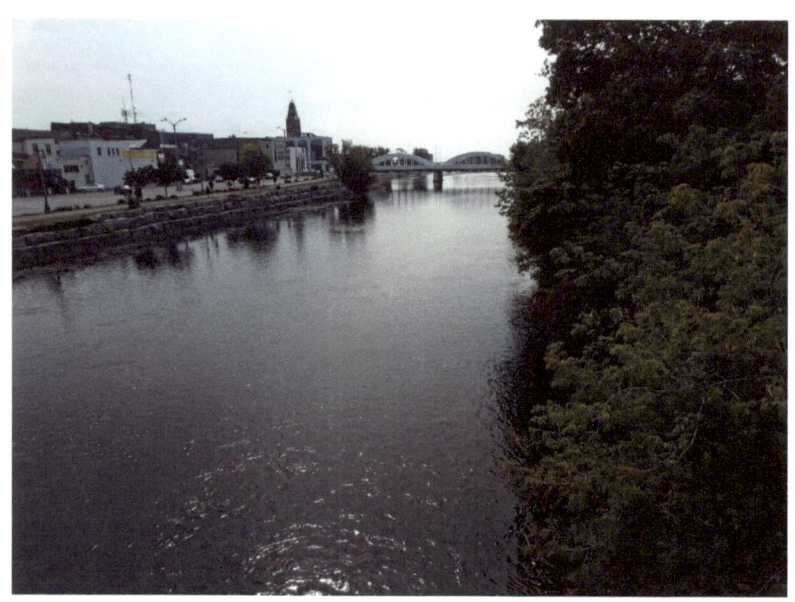

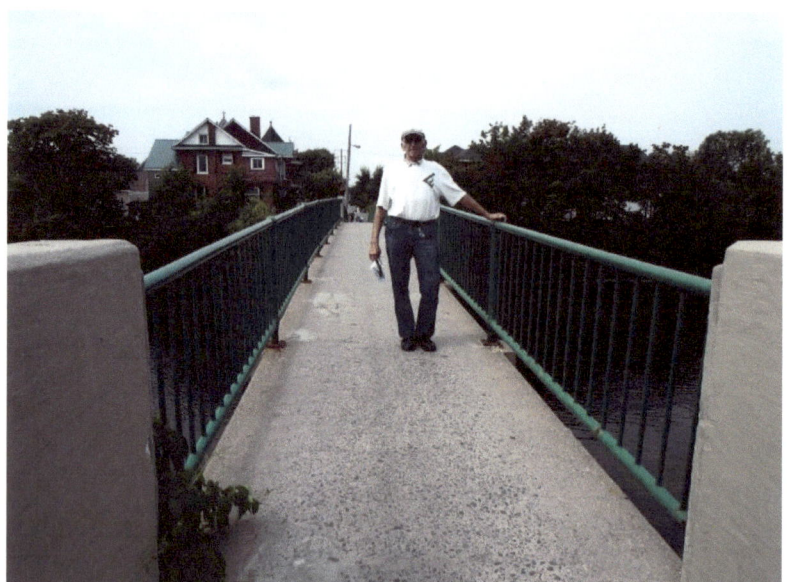

J.B. (Ben) Corke Footbridge – Ben Corke (mayor from 1975-1980) was instrumental in developing the Quinte Sports Centre, and was recognized for his superior financial management skills

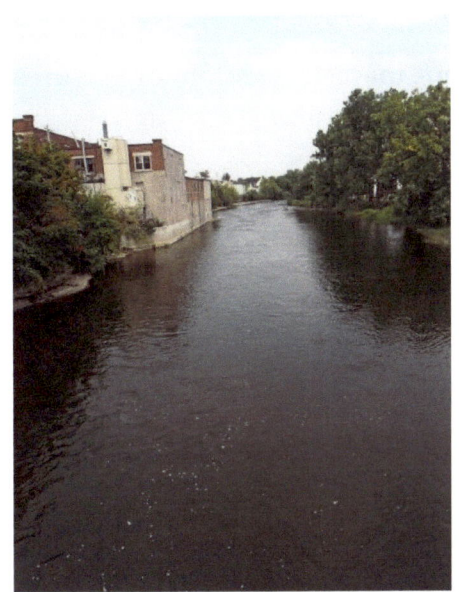

Moira River

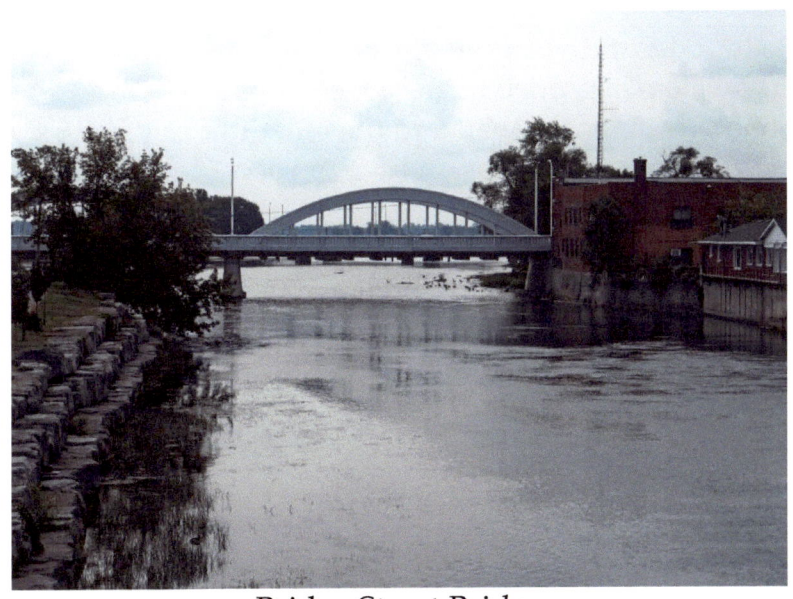

Bridge Street Bridge

Banding: Different materials, colors or textures used in horizontal bands along a wall. Example: 221 John Street, Page 32	
Battlement: A design for a parapet that has alternating solid parts and openings, originally used for defense, but later used as a decorative motif. Example: Church Street, Page 18	
Bay Window: A window that projects out from a wall, in a semicircular, rectangular, or polygonal design. Used frequently in Gothic and Victorian designs. Example: 214 John Street, Page 31	
Brackets: a decorative or weight-bearing structural element which forms a right angle with one side against a wall and the other under a projecting surface such as an eave or roof. Example: 11 Victoria Avenue, Page 26	
Buttress: a masonry structure built against or projecting from a wall which serves to support or reinforce the wall. In Canadian architecture, they are sometimes used for decoration. Example: 201 Church Street, Page 24	

Capital: The uppermost finish or decoration on a column. An Ionic column has a small base, a thin elegant shaft, and a capital composed of volutes which are carved whirls or twists that take the form of a scroll. Example: 219 George Street, Page 42 A Doric column is characterized by a plain column with no base, a shaft with twenty flutings, and a simple capital with a simple entablature. Example: 214 George Street, Page 41	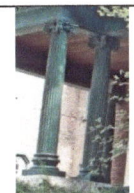 Ionic 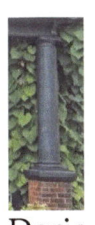 Doric
Cobblestone architecture: Refers to the use of cobblestones embedded in mortar as a method for erecting walls on houses and commercial buildings. Example: 282 George Street, Page 50	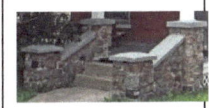
Columns were initially created to support a roof and porch structure. Originally they were free standing. Over time, builders began to build the walls between the columns so that the columns were part of the wall itself. These are called engaged columns. Engaged columns can be either structural or decorative. Example: 296 Church Street, Page 17	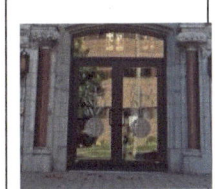
Cornice: originally the wooden overhang of the roof. With the use of stone, brick, iron and steel, the cornice is any horizontal moulded projection at the top of a building. They can be very decorative. Example: 155-163 Front Street East, Page 7	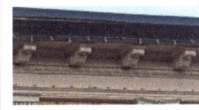

Course: continuous horizontal row or layer of stone or brick. Example: 313 Front Street, Page 12	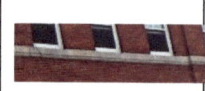
Dentil Moulding: an even series of rectangles used as ornamental decoration in cornices. Example: Front Street, Page 8	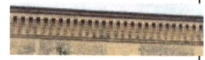
Dichromatic brickwork: the use of two colours of brick, tile or slate to decorate a façade. Example: 202 George Street, Page 39	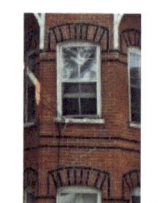
Dormer: (French for "sleep") a gable end window that pierces through the plane of a sloping roof surface to create usable space in the top floor or attic of a building by adding headroom. Example: Church Street, Page 16	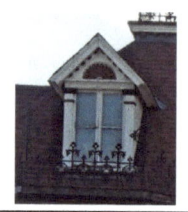
Fretwork: interlaced decorative design resembling a bracket Example: 22 Church Street, Page 23	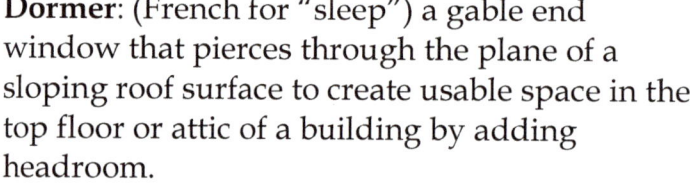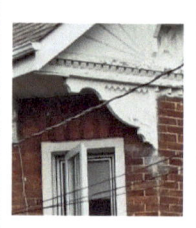
Frontispiece: a portion of the façade of a building, usually a centred doorway that is slightly raised from the rest of the building, usually has extensive ornamentation. Frontispieces are usually Classical in design with white columned porches. Example: 161 George Street, Page 35	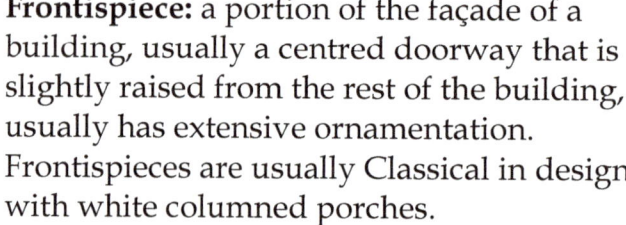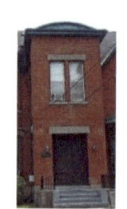

Gable: the triangular portion of a wall between the edges of a sloping roof. Example: 25 Church Street, Page 23	
Hipped Roof: a roof where all sides slope downwards to the walls with no gables. Example: 168 George Street, Page 35	
Iron Cresting: A decorative ornament along the top of a roof. Iron cresting was popular in the Baroque era and also in Italianate, Victorian, Second Empire and Queen Anne styles of architecture. Example: Church Street, Page 16	
Keystones and Voussoirs: a voussoir is a wedge-shaped element used in building an arch. A keystone is the central stone that locks all the stones into position, allowing the arch to bear weight. A keystone is often enlarged and embellished. Example: 242 Front Street, Page 7	
Lancet Window: a tall, narrow window with a pointed arch at its top. Example: 67 Victoria Avenue, Page 25	

Mansard Roof: This style was popularized by Francois Mansart (1598-1666), an accomplished architect of the French Baroque period and especially fashionable during the Second French Empire (1852-1870). This roof is almost flat on the top section, with two slopes on each of its sides with the lower slope at a steeper angle than the upper, and has dormer windows. Example: 200 John Street, Page 28	
Muntin: When a window unit has more than one pane, the material that separates the panes is called the muntin. The larger, more decorative separations are called mullions. In stained glass windows, each piece of colored glass is held in place by a muntin. These were traditionally made of iron. Example: 201 Church Street, Page 24	
Palladian Window: a large window that is divided into three sections with the centre section larger than the two side sections and usually arched. Example: 192 George Street, Page 37	
Pediment: a triangular section above the door or portico, usually supported by columns. The inside of the triangle is called the tympanum. Example: 216 George Street, Page 41	
Pilaster: a slightly projecting column built into or applied to the face of a wall for additional structural support. Example: 155-163 Front Street, Page 7	

Quoin: masonry blocks at the corner of a wall, often a decorative feature, usually larger or of a different colour than the rest of the wall. Example: 280 Front Street, Page 10	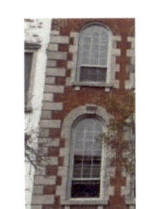
Rose Window: a circular window with ornamental tracery radiating from the centre. Example: 296 Church Street, Page 17	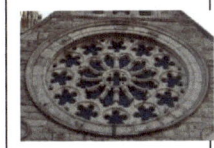
Sidelight: a vertical window that flanks a door, and is often used to emphasize the importance of a primary entrance. **Transom Window:** the light above the doorway, also called a fanlight. Example: 4 Church Street, Page 20	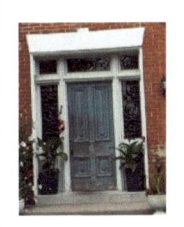
Tower: A circular, square, or octagonal vertical structure higher than the surrounding structure that is usually part of an existing building and is created either for extra defense or for a specific purpose such as a clock or a bell tower. Example: 278 George Street, Page 50	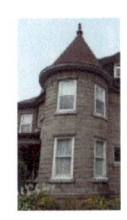

Verge board and Finial: also called bargeboards – hang from the projecting end of a roof and are often elaborately carved and ornamented. **Finial:** ornament added to the top of a gable, pinnacle, canopy or spire – a Gothic element. Example: 214 John Street, Page 31	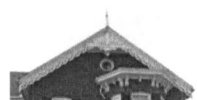
Window Hood: A **hood** is the piece found above window openings, usually of an ornate design, and covers the top third of the opening. Hoods are commonly placed above arched or curved openings on both windows and doors. Example: 155-163 Front Street East, Page 7	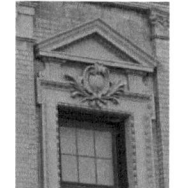

Building Styles

Georgian, before 1860 – This style began with the British King Georges in the 18th century. These buildings have balanced facades around a central door, medium-pitched gable roofs, and small paned windows. Example: 175 George Street, Page 36	
Gothic Revival, 1830-1890 – These decorative buildings have sharply-pitched gables with highly detailed verge boards, pointed-arch window openings, and dichromatic brickwork. It is a common style in Ontario. Example: 296 Church Street, Page 17	
Neo-Gothic (Collegiate Gothic): is monochromatic and on a much grander scale than Gothic. Neo-Gothic was adopted as the style for schools and universities in the early years of the 20th century. The style became so common for scholastic buildings that it is often called Collegiate Gothic. Wall buttresses and finials are added, but they are generally far too small to be of any structural benefit. Example: Belleville Collegiate, Page 19	
Queen Anne, 1885-1900 – This style is distinguished by an irregular outline featuring a combination of an offset tower, broad gables, projecting two-storey bays, verandahs, multi-sloped roofs, and tall, decorative chimneys. A mixture of brick and wood is common. Windows often have one large single-paned bottom sash and small panes in the upper sash. Example: 278 George Street, Page 50	

Renaissance Revival, 1870-1910 - The Renaissance Palazzo was a three or four storey building with a rusticated (very large masonry blocks with deep joints and decorated with rough or bold finishes) ground floor, and regularized understated windows on two upper levels, always finished by an elaborate cornice. The Renaissance saw the development of a graceful and balanced adaptation of the Greek styles. In Ontario, the Renaissance was revived in commercial buildings, banks, offices, and churches in many towns. Most of the Renaissance Revival buildings are designed without columns while those with columns and pilasters are more ornate. Example: Page 6	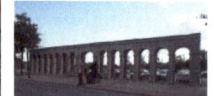
Romanesque Revival, 1880-1910 – This style hearkens back to medieval architecture of the 11th and 12th centuries with a heavy appearance, blocky towers and rounded arches. Example: 201 Church Street, Page 24	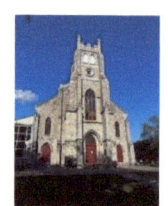
Second Empire, 1860-1880 – The mansard roof is the most noteworthy feature of this style and is evidence of the French origins. Projecting central towers and one or two-storey bays can also be present. Example: 200 John Street, Page 28	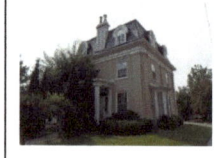

www.ingramcontent.com/pod-product-compliance
Lightning Source LLC
Chambersburg PA
CBHW040843180526
45159CB00001B/304